S0-BHU-680

DISCARD

DON'T MAKE ME STOP THIS CAR!

AL ROKER

DON'T MAKE ME STOP THIS CAR!

Adventures in Fatherhood

With Illustrations by the Author

WHEELER
PUBLISHING, INC.
ROCKLAND, MA

★ AN AMERICAN COMPANY ★

CHESTERFIELD COUNTY LIBRARY

Copyright © 2000 by Al Roker
All rights reserved.

Published in Large Print by arrangement with Simon & Schuster, Inc. in the United States and Canada.

Wheeler Large Print Book Series.

Set in 16 pt Plantin.

Library of Congress Cataloging-in-Publication Data

Roker, Al, 1954–.
    Don't make me stop this car! / Al Roker.
        p. (large print) cm.(Wheeler large print book series)
    ISBN 1-56895-922-2 (hardcover)
    1. Fatherhood—Humor. 2. Fathers—Humor. 3. Large type books.
I. Title. II. Series

[HQ756.R6395 2000]
306.874/2 21
                                                    00-028467
                                                    CIP

This book is dedicated to: Isabel Roker, for bringing me into this world; Al Roker Sr., for being the father I strive to be; Courtney and Leila Roker, for inspiring me to be the best father I can be; and to Deborah Roberts, for making me a husband *and* a father. I can't think of a better combination.

THANKS

I wanted to thank the following people for their help with this book: Dr. Janice Marks, Deborah's ob/gyn; the men who helped us on our journey to have babies, Drs. Majid Fateh and Khalid Sultan; my editor, Trish Todd; my representative, Alfred Geller; and Nancy Van Dis, my production manager.

CONTENTS

DON'T MAKE ME STOP THIS CAR!

INTRODUCTION

First of all, thanks for picking up this book. I feel like the flight attendant at the end of a trip from, say, Cleveland to New York. They give that spiel just before you disembark. "We know you have a choice when it comes to air travel, so thank you for choosing Air Cheapo."

I know when it comes to buying books, you have a choice. Lord knows, there's the latest John Grisham book on the shelf. Or *bam!* A cookbook by Emeril can satisfy your hunger. Suze Orman could make you richer, and Richard Carlson will keep you from sweating something. (When he works out, does he sweat?)

What's my point? My point is, I am glad you chose my book. Perhaps you're flipping through it right now, trying to decide whether to buy it. What will it take to get you to go ahead and reach for your wallet? A free forecast? My putting you on TV when you come down to visit me at the *Today* show?

Sorry, I can't promise those things. The good news is, there are two other morning shows with windows that you can get on if you don't make it to ours. Well, one other. I hear that *Good Morning America* is going off the air and ABC is putting on reruns of *Sea Hunt* to take its place.

The best reason for buying this book is that I think you'll be able to relate to it. I'm a dad, and if you're a father, we can share our dadhood.

And I have a mother, so if you're a mother, well, maybe you can get some insights as to why your husband is such a bonehead. See, my wife thinks I'm a Grade A bonehead.

Are you a single guy? Reading this book will either scare the bejeebers out of you and make you swear allegiance to your single lifestyle, or it will so enamor you of the kind of life we fathers lead that you will want to make a commitment to the woman you're seeing, get married, and raise a family. Pronto.

Maybe you're a teenager. Here's proof that your father isn't the only clueless geek out there. Or perhaps this book will make your own father look great by comparison.

So you see, there is something for everybody here. Did I mention it makes a fabulous Father's Day/Mother's Day/Christmas/Arbor Day gift?

Seriously, I think we all have something to learn as fathers. I think I've always wanted to be a father. It's what I was born to do. Being the oldest of six kids, I felt like a surrogate dad to my younger siblings. I enjoyed being the father figure. When you're the oldest, you get to perform many of the "dad" functions without the responsibility.

Ordering your kid brother or sister around is a definite perk. Having them pick up after you, fetch you a cold soda from the fridge, or perform some menial task you didn't want to do was a real plus. In return, you, as the oldest, could impart much in the way of knowledge and insight. "I wouldn't do that if I were you; Mom will go crazy!" Or, "Go ahead, take the cookies, Mom is downstairs doing the laundry. She won't hear you." Advice like that is better than "Dear Abby" or "Hints from Heloise" any day of the week.

In the ensuing pages, you'll find out how I became a father twice. I consider myself a blessed man. Both of my kids are the best a father could hope for. Each is a beautiful, considerate, loving, and funny child. I am amazed at how much better my life is now that I'm a dad.

Yeah, yeah, yeah. I know. I'm bragging about my kids. What parent doesn't? That's why Sony invented the camcorder. They knew that the main reason people would buy these things would be to videotape every move their children make. Technology marches on, creating new and better ways for proud daddies to bore every person who walks into their family room. For my father's generation, it was slides and grainy 8mm movies. For my generation, it's digital snapshots you can e-mail and Hi-8 video.

I guess that's why fatherhood looked so appealing to me. My dad was and continues to be the consummate father. A teacher, a friend, a buddy, and a disciplinarian, he always made time for each of his six children. I think I can honestly say there were no favorites when it came to his kids.

As I got older, I really came to appreciate exactly what he did for us. Why he worked back-to-back shifts as a bus driver. Why he worked odd jobs on the side. Some might say being out of the house was the only way he could get any peace and quiet. I know better. It was because he wanted the best for his children.

Maybe you want to be a dad. Hey, I know what that's like. I've been there. I enjoy being a dad, but it took a while before I was able to be one.

Eventually, I did. I had to travel a couple of different roads to get there, but it was worth the trip. The destination is two wonderful kids who mean the world to me.

I hope you enjoy what I've written and pick up something useful from it. If not, you could always use another book to make your bookcase look balanced. It has a wonderful cover, no?

WE'RE
PREGNANT!

THE ODDS

Deborah and I had been married for about a year when we decided it was time to try to add to our family. Okay, *I* thought it was time, and begged, wheedled, and cajoled Deborah into starting the process. Look, it ain't easy when both people have busy television careers. If you and your spouse work, you know what I'm talking about. Doesn't matter whether it's working in television or in an office or in an auto shop. Juggling work and getting "in the mood" to start a family is hard work.

We began in earnest in November 1996. The great part about trying to get pregnant is trying to get pregnant. It's basically trial and error, and you figure, how hard can this be? People get pregnant every day. And you just have at it.

But after trying and waiting and trying and waiting, finding out at the end of the month that you're not pregnant can be really difficult. We had been trying to get pregnant for what seemed to be an eternity, yet realistically, we knew it had only been about a year. And when you factor in the days that Deborah was traveling or I was on the road, it really was only six or seven months.

Suddenly the awful truth hits you. You spend a good part of your adult life trying *not* to get pregnant. You're dating, you're married—it's not the right time yet. Now, you decide, is the right time. But then you find out it ain't that simple. Turns out there's a very small window of opportunity to get preggers, and if you miss it...oops.

Deborah's ob/gyn, Dr. Janice Marks, suggested we have some tests done to try to determine what was taking so long. We obviously weren't alone. Three million couples are affected by infertility. Sixty percent of the time, the problem is in the reproductive organs of the female. But for 40 percent of these couples, the trouble lies with the male.

Having been through this before in my previous marriage, I knew the deal. I knew that my "boys" had problems—don't swim well at the deep end of the pool and even if they get to the deep end, there aren't that many of them.

After my tests, I found out that my sperm had 11 million guys trying to get to the deep end of the pool. Eleven million! Considering you only need one guy to make it, that sounds like more that enough. But, alas, the average male can have as many as 50 million sperm trying to get the job done. Even so, we had to make sure the problems weren't just mine. It's almost like being a fertility detective: "Al Roker, Sperm Detective." And those 11 million, as I suspected, weren't the best "swimmers." Their motility was below average.

After performing some initial tests, Dr. Marks did a uterine biopsy on Deborah. The doctor goes in and takes a little snip of the uterine wall to make sure it's okay. Dr. Marks said it's pretty painless. WRONG!!!! According to Deborah, it is *not* painless.

Allow me to digress here. In the pregnancy process, I have come to realize how much of the burden is on the female partner. Look, I'm no dummy. I know the stork doesn't bring the baby and drop it down the chimney. Assuming there are no problems in getting pregnant, the female partner has a lot of work ahead of her. She's got a construction zone going on in her belly. She's doing all the heavy lifting, while the guy stands there like the flagman waving the flag that says "SLOW."

Most of the tests on women are pretty invasive and, at best, uncomfortable. So while I'm the one going on about this, I realized that Deborah was the person who would be bearing the brunt of whatever decision we'd be making in our choice to add to the family.

All of Deborah's tests came back fine. There was nothing wrong with her; the problem was more with me. It wasn't that we couldn't get pregnant, but the odds were stacked against us. That's what Janice Marks told us when next we met. But she did have a suggestion.

She recommended we pay a visit just for a consultation with a group called the New York Fertility Institute. Headed by Dr. Khalid Sultan and his partner, Dr. Majid Fateh, these folks would be the ones to help us in our quest to have a baby. Being a male, I liked the idea. "Hey, here's a problem. Here's two guys who can fix it. Let's meet with them tomorrow."

Deborah wasn't quite that eager. I think part of it was a feeling of failure at not being able to get pregnant on our own. Me, I'm used to failure. After all, I'm a weatherman. Failure can be a good thing, because it leads to trying something else. If it hadn't been for failure at getting pregnant during my previous marriage, I'd never have adopted my first daughter, Courtney. Eventually, after talking with some friends who had gone the same route, Deborah agreed to make an appointment. But first she wanted us to try on our own one more time, and so she called Dr. Marks back. After conferring over the phone for fifteen minutes, we had our marching orders. Well, some kind of orders, but decorum forbids me to tell you what those orders actually were (wink-wink).

I can tell you this much. Dr. Marks helped us determine Deborah's window of ovulation, and I think you can figure out the rest. For three to five days on either side of what she thought would be Deborah's ovulation, it was "Yippee!!! Sorry, honey, but doctor's orders, we have to." Truth be told, some of the spontaneity was being taken away. Perform...NOW!!!

On the other hand, we had Drs. Fateh and Sultan as Plan B if after a couple of months nothing happened. With that "burden" lifted, we enjoyed the next few weeks. What the heck, it didn't matter, we were gonna let Sultan and the boys go to work on us in a month or so. Yippeeee!

THE TEST

Fast-forward to three weeks later. No period. Hmmm. We had held off taking one of those home pregnancy tests because we had done it before and had been sorely disappointed, so why bother? There are few things worse than using one of those tests, getting a negative result, and later that evening watching television and seeing some couple use one in a commercial—happy and laughing because they got two blue or pink stripes or dots. And you got squat. You wanna put your foot through the television set. But now Deborah was late, I mean, really late, in getting her period. Plus, the night before she had had severe cramping, worse than she'd ever had before. I figured, "Well, here comes the period." Nothing. No bleeding, zip!

The next day we agreed: Let's take a test. So, on the way home from dinner, with Courtney skipping through the drugstore, I furtively purchased a First Response pregnancy test. Deborah came out of the bathroom and showed me the test. My God!! There were two pink lines. The test was positive! This couldn't be right, could it? My mind was a jumble. We were pregnant? We couldn't be pregnant. I wanted it to be true, but it didn't seem possible. I wanted to jump up and down, but this could've been a fluke, a mistake. I refused to get excited.

We talked about it, and had decided to take the other test, when my sister and her brood showed up at the apartment. Alisa and her husband were in town from Cleveland. She's a nurse and he's a doctor. If anyone knows about this stuff, they do, both professionally and personally. They've got three kids. On the other hand, this is a woman who, upon finding out she was pregnant with her third child after having given birth only five months earlier, said to me, "I can't believe I'm pregnant again. How did this happen?" I think we know how it happened. You're a nurse, he's a doctor. Figure it out! I decided not to tell my sister yet.

After they left, we decided to do the other test: same result. Oh, man...okay...calm down...we're pregnant...needs confirmation...we're gonna have a baby...I know!

At that moment, I felt such incredible love for this woman. We stayed up for a couple of hours talking about it. What do we do? Are we going to tell anyone?

Earlier in the evening, after the initial shock of the first test, Deborah had called her sister, Janet. Janet is wise in these things. Why? Because she's got two kids and did her share of testing *and* knew how she got pregnant, unlike my sister, the nurse.

WHO TO TELL FIRST

The next day was exhausting. It was just starting to settle in that we were pregnant. All the questions started flooding in. What were we going to do? Who would we tell and when? When were we going to tell my daughter, Courtney (then ten years old), who had ruled the roost for so long?

Courtney is my daughter from my second marriage. I knew that this would be a difficult time for her. For ten years she has been the center of my universe, and I hope me of hers. As with many of her friends, she had to deal with the breakup of her parents' marriage and then her father's remarriage.

In the back of my mind, I knew all of this, but it hadn't been front and center; until now, pregnancy seemed like such a foreign concept. If all went well, this was something she would need to know, sooner rather than later.

Deborah was anchoring *ABC World News Saturday,* and I was going over to drop off Courtney with my folks so she could spend some time with Alisa's kids, her cousins. I didn't want to tell my folks, who might somehow let it slip before I was ready to tell Courtney. Yet for other reasons I wanted to tell my sister Alisa. She is my best friend, and during my rather bitter and painful divorce, she and her family kept me afloat, and also kept Courtney from drowning in a sea of anger and guilt.

Deborah and I both decided that if Alisa could keep a secret—which was tough because she and my mom are very, very close—I would tell her. So I divulged our happy secret to her, ironically, in the room where I had spent my formative years growing up in St. Albans, Queens. She came up to my old bedroom and I told her. She started to cry and was so happy. Only two weeks earlier, at dinner at our place, she had counseled Deborah to pray. Alisa loves her like a sister and only wants me to be happy.

After I left my folks, I drove back into the city. Funny, though Queens is technically part of New York City, one of the five boroughs that make up this great metropolis, those of us who grew up in one of the outer boroughs still refer to the isle of Manhattan as "the city."

I went to a bookstore and picked up two books: *What to Expect When You're Expecting* and *The Girlfriends' Guide to Pregnancy*. I headed up to a little store Deborah likes called Adrien Linford and picked up a beautiful blank journal, in case she wanted to jot down some thoughts or feelings during the next nine months, and some scented candles to have lit and waiting for her when she got back from doing the news.

We met our good buddy Carl Killingsworth during Deborah's dinner break. Carl is one of our dearest and closest friends. Yeah, you guessed it, we told him. I knew that this could jinx things, but when there are people you love, people you know who want only happiness and good things for you, it's hard not to tell them. Carl knew we were getting engaged before Deborah did. Right now, my mother is reading this and thinking, How come Carl knew before I did? These are the problems that come from being honest in print.

Carl started to cry. He was speechless. You have to know Carl. He is a sixty-two-year-old North Carolinian who has lived in New York for the past thirty-five years. I met him at WNBC, where he was in charge of press and publicity. We love Carl. Three weeks earlier, he had come upstate to a small cottage we were renting. While we were sitting on the deck, Carl looked at Deborah and asked, "Are you pregnant?" Well, we were floored. As far as we knew, we weren't.

I headed home after walking Deborah back over to ABC. You think you know how close you are to someone, how much you love that person, then something like this happens, and everything you thought you knew goes out the window. I couldn't wait for her to get home.

When she did, I had some light jazz playing. Candles were lighting her way to the bedroom, and her gifts were on the bed. We just held each other. It was a perfect end to the day.

THE OFFICIAL WORD

August 2, 1997, we went for our first prenatal visit at Deborah's ob/gyn, although I guess she's now *our* ob/gyn. By the time I got there, Deborah was sitting in Janice Marks's office. I kissed her, sat down, and in walked the doc. She told us their test results matched ours, so, at least by these tests, we were preggers.

There was still blood work to be done, but Dr. Marks reached into her desk and pulled out a plastic wheel with numbers written all over it and a window that changed as she turned the wheel. I called it the Wheel of Gestation. It calculated when we got pregnant and when we were due, and the first trimester.

Then Janice told us a statistic we didn't want to hear. Twenty-five percent of all first pregnancies end in miscarriage. So, until we got past the first trimester, we shouldn't get really excited. I started to gird myself for that possibility. I mean, it was amazing enough that we actually got pregnant, given our situation, and then to have it go full term would be a miracle. So we told virtually no one, other than Alisa and Carl, because there was a one-in-four chance that we wouldn't make it through the first trimester, which would be September 25. That would be seven weeks— a very *loooong* seven weeks.

I felt sort of guilty. Deborah would have to make all the sacrifices. She would have to cut down on coffee. Doesn't sound like much, right? Well, let's just say my sweetie isn't exactly a morning person. That cuppa joe kind of kicks off her morning. Alcohol would have to be drastically reduced as well. Granted, my wife is not a lush, but she does enjoy the occasional glass of wine with her meal. Me, I could eat whatever I wanted and however much I wanted and the baby wouldn't be affected. Is this a great country or what?

We left, loaded down with pamphlets, forms, and a good dose of anxiety. Deborah and I had a rare weekday lunch to talk about what went on. We decided to tell our parents in the next couple of weeks...maybe. No co-workers until late October, early November. Certainly not until after the sonogram, which would be in November.

And we had to deal with Courtney. We decided to tell her in early December, because I didn't want her hearing about it from somebody else in my family—a cousin, or my mom. She needed to hear it from her dad and stepmom.

This was a very scary time. I so much wanted for this to happen, but I was afraid to let go with my joy. If Deborah didn't miscarry, then there was the amniocentesis at sixteen weeks. What if it were to show some abnormality? I think it was easier when our folks were having babies. They got pregnant, they dealt with whatever happened, and that was that. They smoked, they drank, they did whatever, and a generation survived. I'm not knocking what we do today, but with *so* much information, maybe we overload.

Right about this time, the University of Alabama football coach, Gene Stallings, was on the *Today* show with his son. John is thirty-five years old and has Down's syndrome. Watching Mr. Stallings talk about his son, I could see the love he had for him. His Down's syndrome didn't get in the way of that. I think right there, at that moment, I knew that we would never get rid of this baby, even if it had Down's or any other condition that might lead a couple to consider terminating the pregnancy.

You want the best for your baby. Is bringing an "imperfect" child into the world the best thing? Or is it the height of selfishness and ego to deny that child the right to be? I prayed to God that we wouldn't have to make that decision, and that if we did, we would make the right one.

TELLING COURTNEY

In the ensuing weeks, our joy turned to fear. Subsequent visits to Dr. Marks bore out two things. First, Deborah's progesterone levels were not rising as fast as they should. Dr. Marks prescribed progesterone pills, but her feeling was that this didn't help a doomed fetus, only a healthy one. And second, the fetus wasn't growing the way it should. Its heart rate was nowhere near what it should have been.

To confirm her suspicions, Dr. Marks sent us to a sonogram specialist. He delivered the news we did not want to hear: the likelihood that this baby would reach term was pretty slim. We left the building with extremely heavy hearts, riding home in silence, only an occasional sob from Deborah punctuating the relative quiet in the back of the cab.

Dr. Marks had been trying to prepare us for this eventuality. Her less-than-enthusiastic assessment of our pregnancy was based on her experience that progesterone levels as low as Deborah's did not bode well.

The weekend of August 15 seemed to go on forever. I had to leave town for a story on the West Coast. But we had talked and talked and talked on Thursday night, then each chance we got during the weekend.

We both decided that whatever happened was God's will. This baby had been conceived against the odds. The ob/gyn didn't think we could get pregnant by the usual means. Then, when we did, she was sure Deborah's blood work would come back subpar, and it didn't. So, the point is, when it comes to some things, Science, with a capital *S*, may not have all the answers.

Deborah talked with a couple of her close girlfriends for support, and they gave her encouragement and some cause for optimism, even if Dr. Marks couldn't. And Deborah continued to take the progesterone to try to boost her levels.

She went in for some blood work, and then both of us tried to keep as busy as we could. Finally, later that day, Deborah called. Her progesterone was up—not a huge jump, but enough for Dr. Marks to say it was cause for cautious optimism. The next step was to do another sonogram...next Monday.

By Labor Day weekend we had been on a hell of a roller-coaster ride. We vacillated between believing there was nothing going on and envisioning a baby growing inside Deborah.

We decided to tell Courtney, who was with us that weekend, in the event that we had to have a procedure done, and Deborah had to go into the hospital. It's funny. You think you can hide things from your children, but they know. And Courtney is a very sensitive kid. That Friday, she asked me what was wrong. "You seem really sad, Dad. What's bothering you?" she queried. I was stunned. I thought I was hiding my anxiety pretty well. No one at work had guessed, and only very few friends and family knew. So how could this ten-year-old have a clue?

So we told her, and she was excited. I'm not sure if she really heard about the baby's possibly not developing. Oh, I repeated it, yet she hugged Deborah, and started asking the really important questions like when, and where will the baby sleep—as in, Is it taking my room? Or, more important, is it taking my place?

We all sat and talked about the fact that this might not work out, but if it did, we'd be very excited, and that we would all need to help bring the baby up, and that the role of Big Sister was an important and pivotal one. I think Courtney was glad she knew. I asked her to say some prayers for the baby and she said she would.

The thing is, I did think there was a baby inside. It just seemed as if this kid had beaten so many odds to get here. I knew it was wishful thinking, but maybe it was also plain faith. I believed, and therefore it would be.

If we got through the weekend okay, then there would be some blood work and a sonogram. Soon we would know if there was anything to see—or, more important, to hear—like a heartbeat.

THE END

We almost made it through the weekend, but that Sunday Deborah began to get cramps. I could see the worry etched on her face. I think we both knew that it was over, that this baby was not going to make it.

But how do you admit that to yourselves? Intellectually you know it, but you can't say the words. You can't form the sentence. Not to yourself. And certainly not to each other.

We were meeting Ann Curry, the *Today* news anchor, and her husband, Brian Ross. We were downtown at a restaurant called America. We got there first, and Deborah said she had to go to the bathroom.

I sat at the table and ordered drinks, all kinds of thoughts running through my head. Would this baby make it? If it did, given all the problems, would it be healthy? Would we want to keep it if it wasn't? And what if it didn't make it? How will we...then I realized that about ten minutes had passed. Deborah was still in the bathroom. What if something had happened? Was she okay? Just as I was about to get up and check, she came out. I had never seen her look so grim. Right then, I knew the answer to all those questions. Our baby was not going to live.

Deborah said she was bleeding much more than before, and was feeling faint. We got up and told the hostess we had to leave...a family emergency. And, in a way, it was. Our unborn family.

In the cab, I called Ann and told them what was happening. I looked over at Deborah and saw that she was crying. It is a horrible feeling to be completely helpless. To know that the thing you wanted most of all is slipping away. Nobody's fault. No one to blame. It just was what it was.

Dr. Marks answered my page and from the sound of her voice, I knew she felt this was the beginning of the end as well. She advised us to wait, and if nothing got worse, we would see her in the morning at the hospital. Well, we never made it that far. Around 2 A.M. Monday morning, Deborah's cramps became so agonizing that I called Dr. Marks, who told us to go directly to the Emergency Room at Lenox Hill Hospital.

The folks at the ER couldn't have been nicer. Two male nurses moved us through the admitting process and got Deborah into a quiet room as quickly as possible, where an ob/gyn resident checked Deborah out until Dr. Marks could get to the hospital. As this young doctor prepared to do a sonogram, what had been our baby came out. I couldn't watch, but I saw a darkish, red mass, and grief started burrowing a hole through my heart.

If I was feeling this, what was happening to her? How do you come back after this?

Dr. Marks showed up and did her best to comfort Deborah, who was holding up as well as could be expected. I watched this woman, who was as excited as could be at the prospect of becoming a mom. I knew in my heart of hearts that she was going to be a fabulous mother. When I would say as much to her, she'd look at me and say, "I don't know how good a mom I'll make. I mean, I'm so neurotic!" And I would always reply, "Hey, that's one of the prerequisites!"

Dr. Marks kept saying to her, "You will get pregnant! By this time next year, or very soon after, we will be back in this hospital, and you will walk out of here with a baby!"

Then it was time for a D and C. They wheeled Deborah away, and I was left with my own thoughts, and with access to a whole battery of vending machines, of which I availed myself. I probably consumed more junk food that night than I had since college.

Then the nurse came and got me, I saw Deborah in the Intensive Care Unit. It was Labor Day, and there was no one else in the unit. Just the nurse.

There was my wife, looking somewhat dazed as the anesthesia was wearing off. A look passed between us, and that was all that was needed. We held hands and I kissed her. For the first time in three months, there was no life growing inside of her.

Deborah had started to think of herself as a mother. She was thinking of us adding to our family. And now it had all changed. It was different for me; there wasn't anything growing in me, except for the emotion of becoming a father for the second time. For her it was both emotional and physical. Her belly had been growing with life. Mine was growing with Snickers and Ritz Bits.

I think that once the diagnosis from that first sonogram came in, I started to distance myself. I was afraid to believe that this was going to work, that this baby was going to live. I guess I was afraid of how I would feel afterward if it didn't.

Deborah always hoped, always believed. I figured, if things worked out okay, I could always get back on the bandwagon and cheer. And now, as I squeezed Deborah's hand, I was left with this despair. Maybe it was *because* I didn't believe, didn't have faith, even though I had prayed to God and asked for his blessing on this child and to make sure it was healthy; maybe my lack of faith was what doomed this baby. I certainly hope not.

After a while, we took a cab home and got into bed. Deborah was holding up extremely well. We were quiet, subdued. There were tears, and holding and hugging, but it was reserved to a certain extent. I found I couldn't cry.

Later, a therapist told us that I, indeed, had probably let go emotionally when we heard the prognosis after that initial sonogram. But I'm not one to cut and run emotionally...or am I? I pray that I'm not.

FUN WITH FERTILITY

Four weeks after the miscarriage we got a clean bill of health from Dr. Marks. She told us that as soon as Deborah got her period, we could start working on making our baby—that would be another two to four weeks.

Ironically, it was our second anniversary. I mentioned that little tidbit to Dr. Marks while Deborah got dressed. I got some good news of my own. She proclaimed that my wife was in good health and had healed well, so we could really celebrate our anniversary night. Yessss!!!!

We hadn't made travel plans for this anniversary because of everything that was going on with the baby, so I had my good buddy WNBC anchor Sue Simmons get us dinner reservations at Jean Georges, the hottest restaurant in New York. Turns out she plays poker once a week with one of the owners. An "all-girl" poker night got us in!

I also reserved the room at the Essex House where we had spent our first night as husband and wife, right after the wedding. My sweetheart was totally surprised, paving the way for us to start working on the baby!

However, we had also decided to take Dr. Marks's advice and seek the help of the New York Fertility Institute. So, on the appointed day in October 1997, we were in a taxicab headed to the offices of Drs. Majid Fateh and Khalid Sultan. Walking into their offices is like walking into a nicely appointed baby factory. And I mean that in the best possible way. Their mission is to get people pregnant. The walls of the reception area are one giant baby album. Hundreds of baby pictures cover every square inch, every color and size. And, as Deborah noted, a fair number of multiples!!

Dr. Khalid Sultan is a graduate of NYU Medical School. He and his more senior partner, Majid Fateh, came from the highly respected and extremely successful Columbia Presbyterian to start a more "hands-on" fertility center. Judging by the walls, and the crowd in the waiting room, they had succeeded.

During our appointment, he explained the facts of trying to start a new life.

As a woman ages, her chances of getting pregnant just from having sex decrease. If you've waited until your late thirties or early forties, although it doesn't mean you won't get pregnant, it sure is a lot tougher. Add to that a male partner whose sperm are a little less than perfect and suddenly we could see why a year had passed before we knew if we could get pregnant.

Even if this was depressing, I really liked knowing what we were up against. Dr. Sultan made us feel as though there was hope. He told us that we could, in fact, get pregnant again on our own. It just would be a matter of time, the odds, and perhaps various levels of assistance.

Deborah could take a drug like Clomid to increase the number of eggs her ovaries produced and improve the chances of an egg's being fertilized. We could combine the drug therapy with what's called an assisted insemination. In this procedure, they take my semen and "wash" it. By screening out the weaker sperm, they get a concentrated dose of sperm and shoot it up into Deborah's cervix, thereby increasing the chance for fertilization.

Then there's the big one. Artificial insemination. You've no doubt heard about this one, but you may not know everything it entails: drugs, daily shots, and sperm "washing" are involved, but also Deborah's eggs are removed, one single sperm is injected into each egg in a laboratory, then they're "hatched" in a petri dish to see how many fertilize. The fertilized eggs are placed back in the womb; ideally, one or more take hold, and BINGO! you're pregnant.

Those were the options Dr. Sultan laid out for us. After hearing them all and listening to the scientific lingo, I'm not sure we felt any more hopeful, but at least we had a better idea of what we could do. We could choose to continue as we had, naturally, without any help. Not a problem, but a thirty-seven-year-old woman and a husband whose sperm are not optimum quality have an 18 percent chance of getting pregnant.

We could try artificial insemination, without the help of any fertility drugs, but that only raises the odds to about 20 percent. Deborah could take Clomid or Pergonal, fertility drugs, and with insemination, that might raise the chances to between 22 and 26 percent.

Then there's the big enchilada: in vitro fertilization. This procedure raises the shot at getting pregnant to between 28 and 30 percent. Of course, there's adoption, and that's 100 percent successful. That one I know, because that's how I was blessed with the most wonderful girl in the world, my daughter Courtney. Though I don't see eye to eye with her mother anymore, for the gift of Courtney I will always be grateful to my ex-wife, Alice.

We decided that the best bet was to start with Clomid. It's a pill, taken twice a day, and there aren't many side effects. Pergonal, on the other hand, is an injection. I would have to give my spouse a needle once a day. It's a natural hormone called FHS, as opposed to Clomid, which is a synthetic version of FHS. The most bizarre part of Pergonal is what it's made from—the urine of menopausal Italian nuns. Seriously! Turns out the company that makes Pergonal is owned by the Vatican. It seems they have an unlimited supply of pure FHS derived from this nun urine. The nuns live at the Vatican as part of a religious order based there.

Pergonal is the high-octane stuff, and very expensive. Hey, somebody's got to make sure the supply line stays open. It would be cheaper to adopt an old nun and have her live with us!

But we went with Clomid to start with. Deborah took the drug for ten days. We tried three times with the Clomid, off and on beginning in October, with no success. It was a frustrating period, to say the least. By January, I started thinking, Maybe it's something I've done or haven't done, and I knew Deborah was having the same thoughts. We tried to keep those thoughts from creeping into our minds, but...what a surprise...we're human.

With that in mind, and with a certain sense of desperation, we decided to move on to the next step. Dr. Fateh suggested that we try Pergonal and a round of in vitro fertilization. After injections of Pergonal, when the eggs that are stimulated by the drug get big enough, Deborah would be knocked out. The eggs would be harvested and put into a dish, where they would be combined with one of my sperm.

For Deborah, it was a feeling of "Oh, God. We're at our last chance." It was exactly that feeling that Dr. Fateh wanted to discourage. We were at a decision point. In my mind, the Pergonal option became our best bet. Not so in Deborah's. She needed some convincing. Dr. Janice Marks came out of the bullpen and proved to be the closer, helping Deborah make the decision to go with Pergonal and IVF.

It would be TWO shots a day! One dose of Pergonal, and *another* shot of a combination of Lupron and Follistim, drugs that work on stimulating the follicles on which the eggs will grow. The latter is a fairly short needle that goes into the thigh, but the Pergonal is a *looong* needle right in da butt! We decided then and there that it might be better for Deborah to come into the office each morning to get her shots. I'm not the squeamish type, but heck, I was afraid this would be one of these things that could come back to, pardon the pun, bite me in the butt. Maybe one day we have an argument, then I have to give Deborah the needle, and maybe I stick her a little too hard. Oh, man. I broke out into a sweat just thinking about the ramifications.

When all was said and done, I did end up giving her some of the shots. As few as possible, but a few nonetheless. Our ten days of shots went fairly well. Then it was time to release the eggs. Just one problem. Deborah, who, as a correspondent, has to travel for her job (that pesky newsmagazine, *20/20,* just insists she travel out of town to do these darn stories—can you imagine?), had to be out of town, in Tampa, Florida, when it was time for the ACG shot, which releases the eggs. Not just overnight, but at 1 A.M., because the eggs have to be harvested before they get out of the ovaries. There was no way my sweetie was going to be able to give herself this shot.

So I called the general manager of the hotel she was going to be staying at and explained the situation. Lo and behold, there's a service out there called Hotel Docs. For $195 they show up at your hotel and do whatever you need. Kind of a medical escort service. Sure enough, at 12:45 A.M., a lovely female doctor came to Deborah's room and Bam! Injection Central.

The next morning, Friday, February 21, my wife came home and we popped up at Dr. Sultan's office at the appointed hour. While she got ready, I had to go into the bathroom and give up a specimen of the "boys." Something I used to be worried about my parents discovering I was now doing in a room made specially for "taking care of bid-ness." Is this a great country or what?

Before the procedure, there were, oh, twelve or thirteen forms to fill out, including acknowledgment that the procedure could, in very rare cases, lead to sterility and even death. Suddenly we realized the gravity of what we were about to embark on. As Deborah read on, I

43

heard a very audible gasp from her. Why? Well, right there in black and white was a little stipulation that was to keep me "sticking it" to Deborah. If her eggs were fertilized, and implanted, Deborah had to start taking a shot of progesterone every day for the next two weeks until we found out if we were pregnant. Guess who was not crazy about this small fact they had failed to mention? Deborah had become my little pincushion, and instead of her coming to the office to get the shots, yours truly was going to have to start giving her the ol' zapperoo in the buttowski!

Two hours later, my sweetie, a little groggy from anesthesia, came out. While she was still recovering, Dr. Fateh told me the good news, we've got five eggs—four really good ones and one okay egg. We had to wait for a call Saturday morning from the embryologist to find out if the eggs became embryos. Had cell division started? This is one big freaking waiting game, and it was beginning to drive me nuts, but I didn't want Deborah to see that I was beginning to crack. After all, she was on the edge, and it wouldn't do for both of us to lose it. That's one of the great things in our relationship. We take turns being the strong one and the needy one.

The other great thing that was emerging from all this was that I think we became far more spiritual. Prayer and thoughts about God became far more important. Too bad it couldn't have happened without the stress and strain of wanting something more than we realized was possible. But, I guess the Lord doesn't mind which path brings you to him, just as long as you get there.

Saturday morning, 8:30, the phone rings. It's Dr. Obasaju, the doctor in charge of embryos at the clinic. "You have three embryos. We'll see you Monday morning." Yikes!!

Dr. Sultan called to make sure we knew about the embryos. I asked him about the quality of these guys. He told me that each day, the embryo's cells should double, from one cell to two, two to four, and so on. Think of the embryos as a delicate soufflé in the oven. The soufflé likes being in the warm, nurturing environment. Keep opening the oven, and the temperature fluctuates; the vibration of opening and closing the door can cause problems, can even collapse the soufflé. Same with the embryos. So the docs wouldn't "peek" until Monday, when they were to be placed into Deborah's uterus. Monday came all too slowly.

I knew that we had two weeks of pure agony awaiting us. Not only did we have to wait to find out if all this took, but I was going to have to take over administering the shots. At least it was down to one a day, but this time, the shot consisted of 1 cc of progesterone in an oil base. With a loooong needle. And you couldn't just zap it in and push the plunger and be out. This was oil, so it took longer to get all the stuff into my wife's butt! Theresa and Millie, the nurses at Fateh and Sultan's, recommended heating the progesterone in hot water to make it go in a little easier.

One of the wonderful things about being with someone you know very well is that after a while, you can start filling in the thought balloons over each other's head. One night, I had just given Deborah the shot and was pontificating about the pregnancy. My darling shot me a look that had something less than love in it. I instantly knew what she was thinking: Oh, sure, give *me* advice about getting pregnant. Why don't you try getting pregnant and get something like hot motor oil shot in your tush and see how easy it is!! I told her what her thought balloon was and we both burst out laughing. It was exactly what she was thinking.

The first week went fairly quickly. Our spirits were good. We had, after much talking and soul-searching, come to the conclusion that perhaps this was God's way of making us take a hard look at our lives and realize how blessed we were even if we didn't get pregnant.

I told Deborah that I didn't marry her because she could get pregnant. I married her because I loved her, and baby or no baby, nothing was going to change that. We talked it up and down and got to a place where we would be able to deal with the disappointment of not being pregnant. We were feeling good about our decision, but it hadn't been put to the test.

Over the weekend, Deborah noticed a little blood. Uh-oh. Suddenly a pall was cast over the day. Here it comes. Her period. There were points in our courtship when the arrival of her period would have meant good news. Not so now. It was the last thing either one of us wanted to see.

When Monday morning came and there was nothing else, we breathed a little easier. The next week was torture. We had agreed that we—I should say *I*—weren't going to question her constantly about how she was feeling, were there any cramps, did it feel like her period was coming on? These were questions that would just heighten our anxiety. I must say, I was pretty good about it.

The weekend passed by relatively quickly, what with having Courtney and my parents up at our weekend place. Then came our last night before finding out if we were pregnant. The answer would come on Monday at Fateh and Sultan's offices with the blood test. The night dragged on and on. Deborah and I talked again about how we would feel if we weren't pregnant.

Deborah had blood drawn early that Monday, March 9, before going to work, so we met for lunch at her office so we could be together when we called for the results. I got there, we kissed, talked a little bit. She took a deep breath and dialed the number. As she dialed, Deborah held out her hand to me. I took it, squeezed, and waited.

"Hi, Millie, this is Deborah Roberts.... Oh, Millie." My heart sank at the sound of disappointment in her voice. "No results? But

Wilson [the lab tech] promised. *What??* Three o'clock?!?" Deborah went on to explain how we wanted to be together to hear the news, and 3 P.M. was much too late. Wilson, a genial and very gentle man from West Africa, got on the line with her, apologizing profusely, and explained that a sudden rush delayed our sample, but that he would have it by 2:15 at the latest, and the sample was going in *right now.*

Meanwhile, I was seething. What the hell was this? Didn't they know what we were going through? Did they have any idea? In retrospect, I'm sure everyone in that office had heard the frustration, the rage, the anger borne of denial of a basic human need: to conceive a child. It is part of our genetic code, our very fiber, that demands we reproduce. And now, just on the cusp of knowing if we had stepped into the role that our parents, and their parents, had, a backup of blood samples stood in our way.

Deborah hung up. We hugged and decided to go out to lunch, come back, and call again. Surprisingly enough, lunch went pretty quickly. We were—and are—luckier than most folks. Just another one of our blessings: jobs that give us flexibility to go to the doctor or grab an impromptu lunch when we need to. We talked about almost everything *but* the pending results. Our jobs, the defining issue in our lives up till now, occupied most of our conversation.

By 2:10 P.M., we were back in Deborah's

office. Her message light was flashing. Checking her messages, one was from Millie at 2:04. I thought, Good sign? They wouldn't voluntarily call if it was bad news, would they? While I was playing my little guessing game, Deborah was dialing.

"Hello, Millie?... Oh Millie!!!" This time her voice was filled with joy and excitement. Deborah squeezed my hand. I got up from the other side of the desk as she came around from her side, and we hugged. Millie was telling Deborah when to come in again, and some other administrative stuff. I realized that I hadn't taken a breath. I let out a huge sigh, and felt all the emotion in our bodies releasing. As quickly as that left, the happiness of reaching the first step of our goal replaced it.

For me, knowing that this would be a long journey, I tried not to get *too* excited, but how could I help it? And at the same time, I knew, as we hugged each other, we were both thanking God for letting us get this far.

We were on the journey. It seemed like forever, but as Deborah pointed out, we found out that we were pregnant exactly six months to the day from when we first saw Dr. Khalid Sultan. The Sultan of Swat had helped us hit a home run our first time at bat with the Pergonal. Of course, this was just the first inning and we had a long game ahead of us. (Don't you hate people who use sports metaphors?)

THE BABY BOYS

Over the next twelve weeks, I started to refer to Drs. Fateh and Sultan as the Baby Boys. We went back to see the Baby Boys to get our marching orders. It was very sweet. Both Millie and Theresa were so happy. Millie told us they were all squealing in the office when the results came in. It was quite touching. Dr. Obasaju came from the lab to give Deborah a hug. Me he ignored, but she got the hug. Hey, I had something to do with this! It's nice to know that this isn't just a business to these folks. It is a hoot to see people whose lives are so enriching. They try to bring a new life to the people who come to see them. But let's face it. The Baby Boys make a good chunk of change here. I mean, just this go-round of IVF and the prescriptions and the ultrasounds and the whole schmear. It's just another way we realized how blessed by God we were to have the financial wherewithal to be able to afford this.

I really believe that insurance companies should foot at least part of the bill for these treatments. It seems somewhat hypocritical to cover the cost of Viagra but not the costs for getting pregnant. To me, it's sort of like buying somebody a new cannon complete with gunpowder and cannonballs, but refusing to give him the match to light the fuse.

As we were sitting in the waiting room to start

the process of blood work and an ultrasound, Dr. Fateh stopped by to grab a quick cup of coffee from a machine behind me, but Deborah had a full view of him. As I was looking at her, I saw her eyes widen, and her mouth formed the question "Two?" I whipped around, and there was Dr. Fateh, grinning like the Cheshire cat.

"What did you just say, Dr. Fateh?" He smiled impishly. "Oh, nothing...nothing. Just the fact that I take two sugars in my coffee." With that, he wandered back into the complex, chuckling, quite pleased with himself. I wondered how pleased he would be if I tackled him from behind and said, "There's one...there's two lumps for your smug little medical butt." But since this was the guy who was helping us have a baby, I decided to hold off.

At that moment, Wilson, the bloodsucker, beckoned and we dutifully went to have my wife's veins tapped for a specimen. She apologized to him for going postal over the phone on Monday when there was a delay on our pregnancy test. I'm sure he'd seen it all before, but he was keeping a wary eye on both of us.

After the blood work was done, we went into the ultrasound room, where Deborah was prepared for our first ultrasound. Both Drs. Fateh and Sultan came in, grinning from ear to ear. They were just short of high-fiving us. Dr. Fateh was working the ultra-sound wand, and as he went in, he noted that the sac that secretes progesterone hadn't formed. It's this sac that produces the progesterone until the placenta is in place, at about eight weeks.

Then, the moment of truth. Into the uterus and there it was. We saw a picture of our baby. It was hard to tell if he had my eyes or Deborah's nose. It was just a fuzzy little black spot, but he or she was there. Our first baby picture. It was hard not to get emotional when we saw it. I didn't know how emotionally invested to get. We had eight more weeks to go before we were out of the first trimester. During those eight weeks, anything could happen. But, with God's help, it would all be okay.

THE DREADED QUESTION

Who knew being pregnant was fraught with such emotional and physical pitfalls? In early May 1998, we came home from a movie screening. I was in my office, which was to become our baby's nursery, doing some work on my website, when I felt a presence.

I looked over at the door, and there was my beautiful wife staring at me with an odd look on her face. I must admit, I didn't notice the odd look at first because I was staring at her breasts, which seemed to grow every day she was pregnant! But eventually, being the sensitive guy that I am, I did notice it. "What's wrong, sweetheart?" I asked, half-knowing and completely dreading the answer.

"My butt is starting to look like cottage cheese, and my arms are getting flabby. I'm falling apart and I'm just five weeks pregnant!" This is a woman who at the time was, and has since returned to being, a size 4, and thinks she's just this side of chubby. This is a woman who runs, boxes, jumps rope, and lifts weights. In short, my wife works hard at being in shape. Why? So she can buy off the rack secure in the knowledge that she looks damn good in any little slinky black number that Ralph or Donna or Calvin can toss off.

I should note here that Deborah went through this manuscript before it was published and made little notations in the margins. Next to the previous paragraph, she wrote, "Makes me sound too vain." I just want to state, for the record, that these are my opinions, not hers. So don't hold it against her that I said "she looks damn good." On the other hand, she didn't say I was wrong, just that it made her look vain.

Now any guy who has been in this dilemma knows that he is doomed. There is no good answer here. If you say, "Awww, honey, you look good to me!" she reads that as, Yes, I am going to hell in a handbag, but you're stuck with me. I'm having your child, so shut up and love me!

If you say, "Sweetheart, you're crazy. You look fabulous!" she will think you are lying through your teeth and you may as well put yourself on a slab and place a sign around your neck that reads "Dead Meat."

So it was with trepidation that I quickly responded, because to hesitate is to die. If you wait a nanosecond too long to answer this kind of question, you get, "You had to think about it, so you *do* think I'm losing my shape!"

"Baby, you look great. It's just five weeks. You can't possibly be losing your body yet. And the fact of the matter is, you *are* in great shape, and will continue to exercise once our doctors tell you it's okay. And after the baby comes, you will be right back at the gym working out and getting back in shape."

I waited for the response...my beautiful wife leaned over and kissed me on the lips. Yessssss! I survived. I lived to see another day.

What my spouse didn't yet realize was that she would get very little sympathy from her sisters-in-arms out there. Why? Because she is good-looking, and a size 4. A female producer friend of mine summed it all up very nicely when she said, "Well, wait till Deborah gets pregnant. I know a number of women, including me, who want to see that cute little waist of hers expand, and then have to work to get it back!"

Nobody wishes good-looking people any harm. But it's like when Superman gets hit with a chunk of kryptonite. You don't want to see him wiped out, but it's good to see the ol' Supe a little vulnerable, so he knows what it's like to be human.

FEELING BAD? THAT'S GOOD!

Here we were at the beginning of April and I was feeling pretty good because my sweetheart was feeling a little bad. I should explain. Earlier that morning, Deborah got up and was feeling a little woozy. Nauseated and with a headache. Two words: morning sickness. It was all she could do to get one cup of coffee down her gullet, when normally she can polish off a couple, no problem. Breakfast was a major effort for her to finish, and keep down.

That made me feel good because, though I know that no two pregnancies are alike, the last time she was pregnant and miscarried, there was no morning sickness. In fact, she talked about how good she felt. This time, morning sickness, and she was constantly tired. No matter how much sleep Deborah got, she zonked out in the middle of the day.

Yessss! Look, I knew it was still a long way from that little one yelling "Look out, here I come," but I thought it boded well for us. Her blood work was good, but reading up on the preggers stuff, it looked like the shots were going to continue for a while. The placenta wouldn't take over from the corpus lutem until the twelfth or fourteenth week, so I would have to keep giving her the ol' needle.

I had planned for us to go to France in September to celebrate our third anniversary. That would have to wait until the following September, since the Baby Boys had already told us they didn't want Deborah to travel at all during her last trimester.

Me, I had to take a trip for the *Today* show. It was the first time we'd been apart since we found out about the baby. When I got home, lemme tell you, the benefits of having a pregnant wife became more apparent. Without being indelicate, I was faced with more of my wife than there had been before. Not just her belly, but her upper deck, if you will, had more real estate to it. This baby was a gift that just kept on giving.

And she was also getting a little poochie. At night, after a meal, it looked like she was swelling, but by morning it would go down to just a little pooch. I picked up for her a couple of pairs of Gap jeans and khakis in size 6. Her size 4 pants were just about a thing of the past.

Overnight, Deborah had been experiencing major cramps, and it was upsetting her. Let's face it, once you've been through the tragedy of a miscarriage, everything takes on a new and frightening meaning. What does this pain mean, why am I getting this cramp?

Poor Deb had dreams about our going for the ultrasound and finding just an empty sac. She woke up several times in the middle of the night to get some Tylenol. I would wake up and ask how she was feeling, but I would drop back off to sleep pretty quickly. I wanted to stay up and share my wife's pain and discomfort, but I couldn't keep my eyes open. I was just lucky Deborah didn't want to kill me as I slept. Well, she probably did, but the pain kept her from getting up and finding a weapon.

We were at the doctors' offices by 9 A.M. This was the moment of truth. The office was a madhouse that morning, with patients piling up pretty quickly. Bea, the office manager, called us into the back for our ultrasound.

This time Dr. Sultan was on his own, with Dr. Fateh on vacation. "Let's see what we have here," he said. I watched the monitor, seeing shades of gray and white undulate and shimmer across the screen, waiting to see them settle down and find their mark. Suddenly, there was a black spot. More than a spot, really. It was now a large dark kidney-shaped area. And in that area was a little white spot. "There's your baby!" exclaimed Khalid. "It looks good. See?" He angled the monitor so Deborah could see it as well from her supine position. "Maybe we can hear the heartbeat." It was clear Khalid was excited—not as thrilled as we were, but he was pleased!

Sultan spun the trackball built into the machine and a bull's-eye on the screen moved on top of our baby. Then I watched as he manipulated the wand inside my wife—searching, moving, and then, from speakers on both sides of the ultrasound machine (made by GE, my parent company, who bring good things to life!), came a rhythmic sound.

"That is your baby's heartbeat. This is very good. Normally you wouldn't hear this for another week. Let's see, you are how many weeks pregnant? Six?" We both nodded. "In two weeks, that sound will fill this room. See that flutter on the screen? That's the heartbeat!"

Deborah and I held hands. Her smile lit up the room and made me so happy. Here was the woman I love, filled with the knowledge that she was carrying a living being inside of her. The doubt and questions she had about herself as a woman seemed to slip into the background as the little pea on the screen made all those problems from before recede.

As he was leaving the room, a beaming Dr. Sultan said, with uncharacteristic optimism, "I'd say you've got a ninety-seven percent chance of this baby making it." It was like a giant weight had been lifted from our shoulders. We left there laughing and giggling. I was so deliriously happy, I didn't even mind giving Lisette, the receptionist, my credit card for payment.

We went down the street to a diner, the same diner we went to when we talked over the choice of whether to do IVF or not. Suddenly, all the people I saw with infants or who were pregnant didn't tick me off or make me jealous. Now I felt good about them, and about us. I couldn't help it.

PICTURE THIS

In early April, I arrived at the Baby Boys' office for a noontime appointment. It was quiet, with only one person in the waiting room.

Both Drs. Fateh and Sultan were there, both relaxed, joking. The sense we got from them was, this baby's doing okay.

We all sashayed down to one of the sonogram rooms, and Millie, one of the nurses, came in. The wand started circling—the moment of truth. It was interesting, because normally, just one of the doctors comes in. These are not big rooms, so we were all crowded around looking at the monitor, with its swishy, fluid shades of white, gray, and black.

Afterward, both of us thought, Something's wrong, they're not seeing anything. They look too serious! Suddenly, there he was. I could see my little peanut floating in a sea of black. A little gray fluttering in the middle. I looked over at Khalid and Majid. They were smiling. "There he is!" one of them proclaimed. "He looks good. Just the right size." One fiddled with the machine while the other manipulated the wand. Deborah and I were smiling at each other.

A flick of the switch and sound was emanating from the speakers. Whereas last time it was bp bp bp bp bp bp, this time it was like this: BUPBUPBUPBUPBUPBUPBUPBUPBUP-BUPBUPBUPBUPBUPBUPBUPBUP!

"Good heart. Right where it should be, about one hundred thirty to one hundred fifty beats per minute. It should sound like a horse galloping," Khalid explained. This kid sounded like Secretariat.

Majid started showing us the head, the body, the heart—there's one arm, there's the other. He flipped another switch, and we saw blood pumping to and from the heart in blue and red and the developing placenta. This was a miracle. I mean, you know it's a miracle, but when it's happening to you, you realize the full impact of the miracle. Just amazing.

Then the show was over, and Deborah was sitting up. They gave us copies of the sonograms for us to keep. Deborah asked about the picture of the day-old embryos they had implanted. Majid smiled and said, "When you bring us a baby picture, we give you the embryo picture."

While I was out paying for this, Deborah was getting her blood drawn. I saw Majid with our file and he was pulling out the embryo picture. Khalid looked over and said, "What're you doing? The deal is a picture exchange!" "She thinks I'm such a hard guy. She's been good. I figure, what the hell?"

60

With that, he handed me the small two-inch-square black-and-white picture of a four-celled organism, along with pictures of the three embryos that never implanted. I slipped it into an envelope and put it in my pocket to surprise Deborah. After she displayed her burgeoning belly to the ladies in the office, we got ready to leave. On the way out, I pulled her aside, gave my wonderful wife a kiss, and showed her a bag. I had been doing a little shopping at Eileen Fisher, the favorite of pregnant Manhattan women. I had picked up a few outfits for her.

We went up to Sarabeth's, a local restaurant, to celebrate. After we gave the waitress our order, I told Deborah to close her eyes. I pulled out the embryo picture. When she opened her eyes, she squealed. "How did you get this?" I explained the story and we laughed. "I feel a little weird," Deborah said. "How do we tell the baby that he or she had a brother and sister, but that they didn't make it?" I hadn't thought about that, but I would worry about it later.

We then had dinner with another couple whose wife was pregnant, ready to drop in two weeks. We shared stories and sonogram pictures. It was good to be in that club. We had been excluded from it for so long. We were savoring the membership. And in seven months, we would join another club, one that lasts a lifetime, called parenthood.

It is a great place to be. Especially after where we had been. It is amazing. And we thank God. Every day.

MATTERS OF THE HEART

So there we were sitting in the office of our ob/gyn, waiting to get checked out by her. It was transition time. At the end of twelve weeks, there would be a handoff, as we went from the Baby Boys to Delivery Doc.

Janice Marks is a wonderful, compassionate doctor whose mannerisms and directness remind me of, well, a toon. She's a small and pretty woman. Yet there's something toonlike in her behavior, which made me instantly like her. She has quick movements. It's like when she leaves a room, you can almost see the puff of smoke and speed lines trailing behind her, with a sharp *zip* or *peeeng!*

When Deborah read this part of the manuscript she said, "You can't call her Toon Doc. She'll be insulted!!" "But, to me, that's the highest compliment you can pay a person," I replied. "Not everybody shares your fanatical love of toons, Al," Deborah answered. My wife once noted, and rightly so, that I would give almost anything to find the portal to Toon Town, as in the classic film *Who Framed Roger Rabbit*.

But Dr. Marks is an excellent doctor, and we were glad to be sitting in front of her. We went through filling out the same forms we had filled out before when we had lost the last baby. It was a weird feeling, déjà vu, a sense of dread yet hope. This baby felt so much different to Deborah, but we still were aware that up to 25 percent of all pregnancies miscarry in the first trimester. So until we hit that twelfth week, there would be nothing we could do but hope and pray.

Janice sat there with the Wheel of Gestation, figuring out dates. Our transition days were Sundays, so the next Sunday would put us at nine weeks. Man, just nine weeks? It seemed like this was dragging on.

We talked about the first ultrasound, the date when we could have amniocentesis done. We still had to address that, because we had pretty much decided that if it were a Down's syndrome baby, we would still keep it. We also knew that amnio has a risk of causing a miscarriage, and if we would keep the baby anyway, why risk it? That said, Janice Marks pointed out that in Deborah's age bracket, an amnio would be advisable if you weren't going to go full term if it had Down's or some other major problem.

Heavy stuff. So much going on. It almost seems impossible that so many healthy babies are born. We moved past that discussion and talked about what Deborah could and couldn't do. Walking was fine, working out was fine, as long as it was with a trainer who had been briefed by Janice. Swimming...great. Deborah could start traveling in the next trimester, providing that she check in with Janice a day or two before she took off. Our due date was November 13. Yikes! A ratings sweeps baby! In this special report, BABIES! You love 'em. Stay tuned!

Then Deborah went in for an exam. After a little time, Dr. Marks called me in. She had this handheld ultrasound thingy. "Well, it's very hard to hear the heartbeat at eight weeks, but let's try anyway."

She pressed the wand on Deborah's belly. Scratchy noises came out of the speaker, then a faint "whoosh whoosh whoosh whoosh." That was just the sound of Deborah's blood coursing through her veins.

Dr. Marks was determined to find our baby. Then suddenly...bup bup bup bup bup bup bup bup bup... "There he is!" she exclaimed. We could all hear our baby. Deborah and I squeezed each other's hand. Janice was all smiles. "Great. He's real! He's in there!" We took this as a very positive sign, because Janice is a very cautious woman. Yipppeeee!

We made our appointment to come back in three weeks. Big changes, she warned us. Big changes coming. Tell us about it.

OUR EVER-CHANGING WORLD

We had been away at our country house for a week, and so it was time to see the Baby Boys. We were very relaxed, serene, and ready to see what had happened to our little peanut in the past two weeks. I know what had happened to my wife.

Her belly was expanding, slowly but surely. This is a woman who prides herself on her body and her shape. She works out, she runs, she watches what she eats. This is a sea change for her. *Welcome to the rest of America, sweetheart!!*

So we went in to see the Baby Boys, but only one of them was there. Majid Fateh greeted us warmly, as did Millie, Lissette, and Theresa. By now, we were all pals. As we walked past Wilson, the blood man, I realized this guy was like the Vampire Lestat, from the Anne Rice novels. He was constantly sucking blood out of Deborah's arm. Okay, he had been using a needle, but I think that's just because people might get a tad testy if he started biting their arms. But at least some good had come out of this.

We had started transitioning over to Dr. Marks, and she wanted to run her own blood tests. I came up with a rather ingenious idea. Rather than have Deborah get stuck and sucked twice or three times a week—by two different technicians or nurses—I convinced them to try something different. Wilson drew several vials of blood each visit, and the Baby Boys' lab ran tests for them *and* ran tests for Dr. Marks. Voilà! I am a genius, no? I'll give you time to sit back down and stop applauding.

Anyway, as Deborah went into one of the examining rooms, Dr. Fateh turned to me and said, "So you graduate today, huh? This is the last examination visit." Huh? What? I poked my head in the door to the room and told Deborah what he had just said.

"Huh? What?" We think so much alike. But it was true. We were at our tenth week. It was time to move over to Dr. Marks. We came back for blood work the next week, but the twelfth week was April 27, and we were scheduled for a sonogram/ultrasound at her place on the twenty-eighth! We had been through so much over here. So much pain, disappointment. Heartache. Hope. Amazement. Elation. It was hard to believe we would be moving on.

Deborah hoisted herself onto the table, assumed the position, and in walked Fateh. He confirmed the diagnosis as to our departure date and seemed a little disappointed as well. But to the task at hand.

The gray fan pattern on the ultrasound machine wobbled, undulated, and took form. There, in an oval of black, in shades of gray, was our baby. Even as I write this, my eyes start to well up. We could see, plain as day, a baby right before our eyes.

"Look, he's sucking his thumb," Fateh exclaimed. "He's a good size. Perfect. Perfect!" With that, he gave us a tour of our child. "There are the orbits, the arms, the legs. Look! Two feet, two hands. The spine. There in the center, that swirling little object...the heart." He then flipped a switch and we saw blue and red swirling around the baby's middle. "There's the heart. The blue is blood moving out, and the red is blood moving in."

It was unbelievable. I looked down and realized that we had instinctively grabbed each other's hands. This was Must See TV. There on the screen was this little figure, kind of like the Dancing Baby from *Ally McBeal*.

I asked Dr. Fateh if the baby was moving so much because of the ultrasound wand moving inside. "No," he assured us, "this is an active baby. Look."

Fateh estimated that the baby was about eleven weeks old. Since we knew the exact day of conception, and counting that and adding two weeks to the first day of Deborah's last period, we came up with ten weeks. This could be a big baby!

"Ah-ha. I know what this baby is!" Dr. Fateh said mysteriously. Deborah and I both looked at each other. What? I knew from my reading that the sexual organs were still on the inside and couldn't usually be seen on an ultrasound at ten to twelve weeks. Theresa looked at the monitor and said, "Oh, I know, too!"

Now I was looking at the screen. I couldn't see anything, other than what he had showed us. We had both decided that we didn't want to know the sex of our baby. There are so few surprises left in life. Why spoil this one? Wait to find out what God is giving us, like our parents did and their parents did. But now...

He clicked another switch and the sound of our baby's heartbeat filled the room. "Strong heart," Fateh said. With that, he hit Print on the unit, and as several copies of pictures scrolled out of the machine, he said, "You are out of the woods." But it's only ten weeks, we said. He shook his head. "Look, anything can happen, but this is a healthy baby."

After Fateh left, we were alone in the room. We hugged. There were still tears in our eyes. We looked down at the pictures of our baby. Our baby. As Deborah got dressed, she said, "Go find out. I don't want to know, but if you do, go ask him." I sidled out of the room, and saw Fateh in the hall. "What is it?" I asked. A smile played on Dr. Fateh's lips. "No! No! NO! I'm not telling you. You told me you didn't want to know and I'm not going to ruin it for you because of a moment of weakness!" He then proceeded to tell me that with his second child, he wanted to know, but their ob/gyn refused, since they had initially told him that they didn't want to know. He thought, Hmmmm, good policy! And so ever since, once a patient says they don't want to know, there's no changing back.

It was a very, very special day. Our pea had turned into a peanut. And we'd been turned to peanut butter.

KEEP ON GROWING

Having graduated from the Baby Boys, it was on to visit the offices of Dr. Janice Marks. Within a few minutes, we were whisked into an examining room. My sweetie got on the scale and it read 131 pounds. She was up six pounds since her pregnancy had begun. She was bummed. Most of America would kill to be 131 pounds. But that's my Deborah!

Deborah was up on the table, and the nurse squeezed some of that aqua goop onto a hand-held Doppler device to hear the baby's heartbeat. She started moving the wand around Deborah's belly. Lots of scratchy noises, a little sound of my wife's blood flow...but no heartbeat.

Okay, don't panic, I kept telling myself. But after five minutes, the nurse said, "I'll let Dr. Marks find it," and left. What the hell was that?? Deborah looked over and saw that my face was ashen and tried to calm me. "It's okay, sweetheart. Everything is okay. Remember, Dr. Marks said it was rare to hear the heartbeat as early as we did, and that normally you don't hear it until ten to twelve weeks!"

Bulldinky! Where's that baby's heartbeat? Gimme that thing. I'll find it! Of course, I didn't say that. "You're right, I know." But inside I was thinking, Where's that damn Dr. Marks? GET THE HELL IN HERE!!!

Just then Janice walked in. She is so sweet.

I've already mentioned she looks like a toon. And I mean that in the most complimentary way. Toons are my heroes. If I could be more toonlike, I would. It's one of my goals.

Anyway, she said, "So, I hear there's an elusive heartbeat!" First she examined Deborah and proclaimed that her uterus was expanding nicely. Deb said, "I can feel it." It was not news to her! Then Janice started running the Doppler wand over Deb's belly.

After a minute or two, my wife mentioned that she hadn't urinated beforehand. "Ahhh," said Dr. Marks, "that explains it. Go empty your bladder! When I was pushing down, something was pushing back." With an empty bladder, BINGO! Janice found the heartbeat. Deborah and I held hands.

After checking Deborah for discharge, which Janice said was normal and would get heavier during the pregnancy, she said, "Congratulations, you are a normal pregnant woman."

After the exam we sat in her office, talking over the mundane but important details. For example, Dr. Marks told us we could start telling people about the pregnancy if we wanted to. We could do most things, but much to Deborah's consternation, she had to wait until mid-May to start working out again. She was chomping at the bit. What a wacko, huh?

We also went over the issue of amniocentesis. We already knew that we wouldn't terminate a Down's syndrome baby. Janice seemed okay with our decision not to do the amnio. In lieu of that, we would have to do a major sonogram at sixteen weeks, which would be in early June. There would also be a blood test to determine if there were any other problems.

We were in our thirteenth week. That meant we had made it out of our first trimester. It was really rather scary. Deborah was now just a regular pregnant woman, and now we were in the capable hands of our little Toon Doc. Whenever we had a question, Janice was there with an answer. Could Deborah start flying again for her job at *20/20*? How about a sip of wine or a nonalcoholic beer? Could she take warm baths? Could she yell at her husband for some minor relationship infraction that really didn't amount to a hill of beans? By the way, the answers were yes, yes, yes, and YES!

The most amazing thing though was the physical change in Deborah. She finally broke down and purchased some stuff in size 10. Much bigger than a size 4, and maternity clothes, here we come! But on the upside, we discovered this cute little company called Belly Basics. They make a thing called "Pregnancy Kit in a Box." It's a four-piece ensemble that consists of a little black maternity dress (there are other colors), shorts, pants, and top. They're elastic, washable, very chic, and $149 for the box. Pretty reasonable and adorable.

We slowly started telling people we were pregnant. Although it's true that a lot of people had been wondering as they'd seen Deb's wardrobe changing from formfitting suits to looser, less constricted clothes, folks around *20/20* had been reluctant to say anything. I hadn't said anything to anyone over at *Today*, except for our executive producer Jeff Zucker, whose wife, Caryn Nathanson, is best buds with Deborah. In fact, she was pregnant at the time we lost our baby. Caryn had just delivered a beautiful boy named Andrew. We also shared our news with best friend Ann Curry and her husband, Brian. They were both in our wedding and are a big part of our lives.

This was becoming more and more real. We hadn't told Courtney yet. Because of a series of scheduling problems, holidays (Mother's Day), and Courtney's birthday, we wouldn't see her until the evening of her birthday on May 14. We didn't want to tell her on Her day, so we decided to wait until Memorial Day weekend to give her the news.

Every night we would talk to Deborah's belly. I told my baby how loved it was, how much we were looking forward to seeing it, how wanted it was.

Sometimes, Deborah would just sit in the family room, pants undone, rubbing her belly, looking down in disbelief. It was a truly amazing sight. I had done the same thing after a big meal, but it just didn't have the same effect.

BABY DECOR

After five months of pregnancy, we were more than halfway home. And *home* was a very appropriate word. With Deborah's health never in doubt, and subsequent sonograms showing a healthy baby, we were concentrating on the accoutrements that would accompany this little bundle.

We were sent by various friends to a place in Manhattan called Albee Baby Carriage. It's a combination Toys "R" Us, warehouse, and Middle Eastern souk for baby stuff. The doyenne of the place is a woman named Annie. A voice made husky by cigarettes and nonstop talking to expectant parents in person and by phone greeted us as we walked in the door. "Hiya, hon. What can I do for you?"

For the next two hours, we were overwhelmed by all the stuff we needed. Now mind you, I'd been through this before with Courtney, but this was Manhattan. In the 'burbs, the choice of stroller, crib set, and linens didn't seem quite so critical. In Manhattan, it is social suicide to be seen pushing anything less than a Peg Perego Milano stroller, although I'm sure by the time you read this, another model will have taken its place in the statusphere.

Annie advised us what to buy and what to put on our "wish list" for the myriad of baby showers that were to be thrown. We had several sets of well-wishers who wanted to toss showers for us. I was amazed at how lucky we were to have such good friends and family who wanted the opportunity to buy us stuff.

By the time it was all over, our heads were spinning. We thought we were a little early for ordering the bedroom set. After all, the baby was due in mid-November, and here it was only July. Uh-uh! This set takes five months, another set we liked took four months. We were getting in just under the wire as far as ordering was concerned.

Then there was the nursery itself. It had been my home office. I had my computer, my files, my books in there. It was my sanctum sanctorum. My Fortress of Solitude. Sorry, tubby. It's all gotta go. We've got a baby to put in here. So now we were looking at paint colors and carpet. What do you do if you don't know whether you're having a boy or a girl? Go neutral. So we were looking at beiges and off-whites and yellows.

This is another area where Deborah wished I was a little more like most other husbands. Most guys I know couldn't care less about the decor of the baby's room. As long as their wives don't break the bank—hey, knock yourself out. Not me.

I wanted in. I wanted to be in on the paint color, the carpet, the bumpers in the crib, the whole megillah. I figure, if I'm going to be in there day in and day out, changing diapers, putting on onesies, and hosing crayon marks off the wall, I should like where I'm going to be spending a huge chunk of my time.

I was driving Deborah crazy. We went through paint-chip charts and wallpaper books by the gross. We looked at swatch after swatch of carpet. Finally, as we were coming out of a paint store, Deborah made a very cogent point. She grabbed me by the shirt, pulled me close, and said, "I'm having the baby, I'm choosing the colors. Get it?"

Well, once she made such a compelling argument, I had to agree. That, plus the homicidal look in her eye, convinced me that she should have the final say on decorating issues.

In the end, we decided to do a sponge-paint on the walls with a mural of nursery rhymes as a border, and stars on the ceiling. When it was finished, I looked around the room and it brought tears to my eyes. It was a wonderful room that was full of love. All it needed was one special addition. Our baby.

THE GUESSING GAME

At six months, the predominant question we were being bombarded with was: What were we having?

In my heart of hearts, I just knew we were having a girl. Call it father's intuition, call it a guess, call it a gas bubble. I wasn't basing this on how Deborah was carrying or the time we conceived or any of that stuff.

I just felt it. Whenever I put my hand on my wife's belly, I could feel this was a girl. When I sang to my unborn child, I got a girl "vibe." Maybe it's because I'm a "girlie-man," in touch with my feminine side.

So when people would venture a guess as to what the gender of our child was, I just smiled. They might be guessing but I knew!

That didn't stop people from speculating. In fact, I think gender-guessing is one of the great true participatory sports today. Anybody can play as long as there's a pregnant woman who hasn't discovered the sex of her child. Doesn't matter whether or not you know the pregnant woman in question.

Walking down the street, we would encounter total strangers who would look at Deborah's belly and say in passing, "Oh, you're carrying like it's a boy. Is it?" We'd shrug our shoulders and just keep walking. Standing at a corner, waiting for a stoplight, we were next to an older couple. The woman looked at Deborah and said, quite proudly, that Deborah was carrying just like she did and that she had had a boy. I responded by saying fetal position had nothing to do with the gender of the baby, that it was just an old wives' tale. The gentleman looked at me and said, "Better listen to her. She's an old wife." She shot him a look that said if he wanted to get much older he had better shut up.

A subset of this was the absolute comfort people unknown to us had in placing their grimy little hands on Deborah's belly. What is that? What gives folks a license to do things they would never do or say to a nonpregnant woman?

I can't tell you the number of times people would tell Deborah either how small she was or how big she was getting. I understand that a person is trying to make conversation, but HELLO!!! I especially loved when someone would tell her she was really starting to show when they were a little on the hefty side themselves. I would hold my tongue, but I wanted to say, "Yeah, she may be big now, but in six months, she'll be back to a size four. How about you?"

We went to a Roberts family reunion in Houston at the home of one of Deborah's sisters. Deborah is one of the thinnest of the Roberts girls. I knew that they were waiting for my wife to get pregnant.

Why? Well, first and foremost, they knew that she wanted to have a baby and were ecstatic when they learned the news. But there was that little issue of weight as well. It was one thing for Deborah to be a size 4, naturally, but maybe she might have to come down and join the other mere mortals who struggle with their weight once she had a baby and was nibbling at the baby's food while feeding him or her.

Imagine their disappointment when they saw her. Deborah really hadn't put on that much weight. Her face wasn't swollen, her wedding ring still slipped on and off her finger with ease, and she wasn't wearing actual maternity clothes, just clothes in size 10 or 12. One of her sisters summed it up best upon seeing her: "Shoot! That's all you've gained? I thought you'd be bigger by now!"

HOME STRETCH

As we entered the final trimester, we realized that there was still much to be done. While the nursery and a lot of the physical stuff had been completed, now was the time to start what almost every pregnant couple goes through...Lamaze classes.

Now, I am generally one of those folks who don't like to do private classes. I like the atmosphere of a group. But on this occasion, I decided that it was probably a better idea to go the private-session route. All I needed was some joker next to me, giving me a hard time about the weather, or kidding me about blowing Deborah's due-date forecast.

Can I be perfectly honest with you? We did three two-hour classes, and the only thing I remembered was the "breathing thing." And I was even a little shaky at that. When did the short, quick breaths come and when were the long, stretched-out breaths? Oh, and weren't these really for Deborah's benefit and not mine?

We had a wonderful Lamaze instructor who guided us through the whole process, but I kept thinking, When do we get to the good stuff? When do we actually do this? I would find myself practicing the whole idea of Deborah's water breaking and rushing to the hospital and going through this process of coaching her through the delivery. I wasn't gonna be one of those nitwit husbands who panics when crunch time comes. Uh-uh.

Then the instructor would ask me a question about something she had told us just five minutes earlier and I would draw a blank. Hmmmmm. That can't be good. So I started taking notes. Hey, I would do that if I were working this as a story for the *Today* show. I would take copious notes. Until the instructor pointed out that if I relied on notes, what would happen if we had to rush to the hospital and I forgot the notes? I'd do like I did in high school...I'd write them on the soles of my shoes and cheat!

The fact was, this baby was coming one way or another, whether Deborah and I remembered our breathing or not. Being the typical male who likes being in control, I latched on to an aspect of the delivery I could handle. Our instructor suggested bringing a portable stereo into the labor room so that I could play music during the labor to soothe and relax my spouse. Cool. Having been a disc jockey during my college days, I immediately warmed to the task. I went through our CDs and started programming the CD player to record "Music to Have a Baby By." When all was said and done, I had amassed eight hours of music. By the time it was over, I felt like giving the time and temperature between each song. "All right, it's fifty-three degrees and Deborah's in her third hour of contractions. This one's going out to our baby... 'Doin' It All for My Baby' by Huey Lewis on Hit Radio WBABY!!!"

Then there was the issue of the baby's name. What were we going to call this little girl or boy? As I said, I knew this was a girl. That was my story and I was stickin' to it. I was Don Quixote tilting at gender windmills. But we had to look at both male and female names as we began the task of deciding on one.

Having learned from family and friends, we decided there was no way we would actually tell anyone in our family what the name was going to be until after the baby was born. Why give 'em time to start complaining and putting in their two cents' worth about what they thought of the name? My feeling is, unless you're paying for the child's braces and college tuition, you don't get a say in the matter.

Deborah and I had decided that it would be nice to honor our respective families by choosing a first and middle name from each. In reviewing the catalog of names, we came down to four. If it was a girl, it would be Leila after my maternal grandmother, and

Ruth for a middle name, after Deborah's mom. If our baby turned out to be a boy, he would be named Benjamin, in honor of Deborah's father, and Charles after my maternal grandpa.

We were pleased with those names and figured everybody would get a little something out of it. Of course, as Deborah pointed out, we missed my father's side of the family. But his side gets the name Roker thrown in there until she—if it was going to be a she—gets married...so everybody's happy!

In the meantime, there was Courtney. For the longest time, she'd been the princess of the house. Having been the oldest of six kids, I always fantasized about being an only child, not having to share a room or a bathroom or a bike with another kid. I never thought about the downside to being an only child. Loneliness is your playmate and it can't be a lot of fun. But even if you wish for another brother or sister, when the reality of a new sibling hits, it's got to be tough.

Courtney was involved every step of the way in this pregnancy and we tried to make sure she didn't feel left out or diminished by the impending birth. I have to give her credit. If it had been me, I would've been milking this for all it was worth and trying to get whatever I could out of it. All Courtney did was try to understand the process and show a lot of interest in both the biology of pregnancy and the emotions surrounding it.

Courtney made it clear that the minute

Deborah went into the hospital, she wanted to be there. Now, while I know that the major part of this concern was because Courtney wanted everything to work and was looking forward to being a big sister, there was another part of her that wanted to make sure everyone knew that this new bundle was second in line. She was top dog, the big cheese, Number One, head of the class. And who could blame her?

And I knew that she had already picked out some clothes for the baby with her mother and a couple of toys as well. It made me love my Courtney more than I ever did. A few weeks went by and issues of a more practical nature came up.

"Dad, where is the baby going to sleep?" Courtney asked one day while we were having dinner. It caught me off guard because she had seen the work going on in the back room that was to be the baby's room. She had gone with us to pick out nursery furniture, accessories, and bedding. So I was surprised. "You know where the baby's going to be, sweetheart. The baby will be in what used to be my office." "Ohhhh, right. So I won't have to share my room." Ahhhh. Now we get to the crux of the matter. "No, sweetie, you get to keep your room to yourself."

I didn't get a room to myself until my sophomore year in college. There were six kids and two adults living in our small, semi-detached house in Queens. Three boys, three girls. You do the math. When I was younger,

I always thought it seemed unfair that Mom and Dad had a room to themselves. I mean, here we were, three to a room, and their room, which was the biggest of the three, only had two people in it. And just one bed! What was *that*?

I always thought my parents were going to be heartbroken when I went away to college. That is, until I saw them boxing up my stuff a few weeks before I left for school upstate. They took apart my bed, emptied my dresser drawers, and moved everything down into the basement. Don't let the door hit you in the butt.

For much of Courtney's life, she was, for all intents and purposes, an only child. She has a brother who is eighteen years older than she is and was away at school for most of her early childhood. Now, suddenly, she had to deal with a little sister.

It's something I never had to deal with. Although I will admit, when my mother was pregnant with my youngest brother, Chris, it was traumatic. Three of us siblings are biological, and three of us came through foster care. I'll never forget coming home from school one day during my sophomore year in high school. I walked into the kitchen and Mom was sitting at the table.

She had a funny look on her face as she asked me how I felt about another little brother or sister. "That's great, Mom," I said. "So we're adopting a little kid?" She shook her head no. "So then we're taking in another foster child?" Again, the head indicated no. So, if she and Dad weren't adopting and they weren't taking in another foster kid, then the only way... OH MY GOD!!! That meant my mother was pregnant. I don't know about you, but when you're a high school sophomore, the last thing you want to think about is your folks doing...it.

All I know is that a year and a half later, since our baby's birth, Courtney has been the model big sister. She feeds, dresses, and bathes the baby, and even changes diapers, including the ones that are environmental disaster areas. She loves her sibling and relishes the idea of being a big sister. I think Courtney digs the idea that there is someone she can mold early on. Possibly as a potential butler or hand-maiden.

SPECIAL DELIVERY

It was Monday, November 16, 1998. Deborah was scheduled for a checkup with Dr. Marks. There was a good possibility that she would induce labor, since we were now almost a week past the due date. Our baby had other ideas.

Deborah woke up that morning with a wet spot, pretty sure that her water had broken. Later that morning, when Dr. Marks was examining her, she snapped off her latex gloves and said, "I want you both to go immediately to the hospital. Do not go home first; do not stop for lunch. Go directly to the hospital and check in!" Uh-oh. It seemed like everything was okay. Deborah hadn't started feeling major contractions, so what was the problem?

The problem was that once the water starts breaking, the clock starts ticking. You have twenty-four hours to get the baby out, or you run the risk of infection and other complications. So off we went to the hospital, a five-block walk from Dr. Marks's office. Deborah insisted on walking, since she wasn't going to be able to work out. You see what I'm up against? Me, King of the Couch Potatoes, married to the Queen of Fitness. Here she has a perfectly good excuse to take a cab and she wants to walk.

Once we got to the hospital, our check-in went pretty smoothly. Within fifteen minutes, Deborah was in a room on the maternity floor, lying in bed, hooked up to a fetal monitor and an IV drip. Boy, these people work fast. Within the hour, Dr. Marks was there, and had examined Deborah. It was her judgment that the baby was still a long way from being ready to come down the chute, meaning that I could go home and get the bag we had packed and be ready for Deborah's delivery.

I didn't want to leave, for fear of something happening, but Deborah told me to go. "Besides," she said, "I will probably be sick of you by the time this is all over, so get out now while the getting is good!"

Unlike my wife, I took a cab home and back. Grabbing the bag and the boom box with the eight hours of music tapes I made, I had a sense that life as I knew it was about to change. It was a change I had been anticipating and praying for for so long. Now that it was just about here I felt anxious for the first time.

Am I going to be a good dad? Is Courtney going to take to her new sibling? Will Deborah's delivery go smoothly? Will the baby be healthy? Will I be able to pry the baby from its mother's clutches once it's born? Serious questions, to be sure, but the answers were all going to have to wait until after the baby was born.

By two in the afternoon, we were settled into what they were calling at our hospital the LDR: Labor/Delivery and Recovery Room. You and your spouse stay in the same room to go through labor, delivery, and the recovery. It minimizes the shuttling from room to room during the process. I guess it also cuts down on the potential of misplacing father, mother, or baby. If we all stay in the same room, we all know where everyone is. Calls were made to family and a few select friends to let them know where we were and what the deal was. Then we pretty much severed communications with the outside world. The one exception was Courtney. She wanted to be there when the baby was born, but we agreed on her brother bringing her to the hospital Tuesday evening to see her new sibling.

It then became the waiting game. Like most guys, I saw this as a chance to really utilize the technology at hand to record these moments. I was loaded down with a camcorder, a still camera, and a digital camera, and the attendant power cords, attachments, and film that went with it all. There was no way this baby's arrival was not going to be recorded for posterity.

By 6 P.M., Deborah's contractions had started in earnest. But upon examination,

Dr. Marks found that her cervix had barely started to dilate. She predicted we were in for a long night. And she was right. I hate doctors who are always right. We passed the time talking, listening to music, and discussing the reasons for the demise of the lambada and the macarena.

To move things along, Deborah was given a dose of the drug Pitocin to help the dilation. By 11 P.M., it hadn't really worked. The cervix had dilated only by 1 centimeter. Dr. Marks told us we had to reach 10 centimeters before the bell would ring "Done" on the baby microwave oven.

Deborah was a real champ. It was now 1 A.M. and she had held off having an epidural to deaden the pain. Had it been me, I would have had the drugs in and running at check-in down at the registration desk, but she wanted to try to do this naturally. Me, I don't get the whole "natural" vs. "unnatural" thing. If you can have the baby and it can hurt less, go for it. But we were told that the epidural makes it harder to push, so Deborah opted to forgo it as long as possible.

It was pretty amazing, though, watching and listening to the fetal monitor hooked up to Deborah's belly. As the night wore on, her contractions were getting stronger and closer together. They were about ninety seconds apart, yet her dilation was moving like molasses. Ann Curry told Deborah the contractions were like riding waves. You just had to ride the wave.

Well, Deborah was hangin' ten with the best of them. The interesting thing was that I could see the contractions coming on the monitor before she could feel them. So we would go into our breathing mode. I told her, "Okay, sweetie, here it comes…start the breathing." And darned if she wouldn't hold her belly and say, "Oooooo…this is a big one." And she would start breathing.

All the while, I was changing tapes in and out of our boom box, trying to keep her energy and spirits up. I was hoping that suddenly Deborah's cervix would pull an Ali Baba and just "open sesame," but it didn't seem to want to cooperate. Where's the WD-40 when you need it?

By 2 A.M., Dr. Marks insisted that Deborah take some Demerol, if for no other reason than to get some sleep. Her latest examination showed that we were still stuck at 1 centimeter. Not only that, but in feeling the baby's head, she discovered that while the baby was in the birth canal, it was facing up. That would make for a more difficult delivery. Janice's feeling was that if, and it was a big "if," we were going to deliver vaginally, it wouldn't be until 7:00 or 8:00 in the morning. Deborah would need her rest.

What I like about Janice Marks is that she doesn't gild the lily. She pretty much calls it as she sees it. Deborah, on the other hand, wants as much gilding on the lily as possible. She did not want to think about the possibility of a cesarean birth after nine months of carrying this baby. I understood that. It's like running a race and just before you get to the finish line, you're suddenly carried over by a surrogate runner. You finish the race, you get credit for the win, but it doesn't feel the same. Actually, I can't relate to either situation. I don't run, and I can't get pregnant.

By 3 A.M., Deborah was sleeping. The contractions were still coming, but at least she could get some rest. As I watched this beautiful woman sleep, I couldn't help but cry a little. She had gone through so much, and in my heart I had the feeling that this baby would not be coming down the chute, but rather out a new trapdoor. I knew how much this all meant to Deborah.

We were both awake by 5 A.M. and the contractions were really close together. I had stopped taking video by now and had let the music lapse as Dr. Marks came in for another exam. It was at this point that the reality of a C-section had sunk in for me, but not for Deborah. Even though she was still only 1 centimeter, she held out hope. But as Dr. Marks pointed out, the clock was running out; twenty-four hours after the water breaks there is a risk of infection. And as much as we wanted a vaginal birth, we really wanted to be able to lay our baby on Deborah's chest and have it find its way to her breast to start the suckling and bonding process. If the baby had an infection, that wouldn't be possible, since it would be placed in the Neonatal Intensive Care Unit. We wanted to avoid that at all costs.

We all agreed that we had a couple more hours before the decision had to be made, but by 7 A.M. we would have to make the hard choice. On the other hand, as long as this was to be a happy baby, so be it. A C-section baby has its advantages. It doesn't get the "cone-head" look from sliding down the birth canal. There's a lot less trauma involved and no tearing for the mom in that nether region, which meant inflatable doughnuts and sitz baths could be avoided.

Eventually, we had to make the decision. One last examination confirmed that this was the most stubborn cervix in the history of obstetrics. This thing wasn't budging. It was still at 1 centimeter. That was its story, and it was sticking with it. Deborah was still resisting the idea of having a C-section. I asked Dr. Marks if we could have a moment alone. Deborah and I talked and hugged and held hands. In the end, she decided that it was the best thing for the baby. We called Dr. Marks in, and told her we were ready to proceed with the C-section.

I have to pause here for a minute. I'm sure many women reading this are thinking What's this "we" business? I know "we" weren't actually giving birth to the baby. Deborah, in fact, was the only one giving birth, but think about it. This is how we dads keep ourselves in the game. If you want to feel a part of this whole process, you start referring to this as a "team" effort. After conception, we guys are biologically left out, and we need to get in the game. So it's the royal "we." Like the song says,

"Put me in, Coach, I'm ready to play...hey... hey!"

Since I was going to be in the room when the baby arrived, a search was begun for some surgical scrubs that would fit. Hey, you can't tell me there weren't any fat doctors at this hospital. Finally, success! A pair of XXXL scrubs were found, so I shimmied into them, then placed a hairnet on my head. That seemed somewhat useless, given the state of my hair, but hey, rules are rules.

After explaining the process and where the incision was to be made, Dr. Marks had Deborah wheeled to the maternity surgery suite where the C-section was to be performed. As I walked alongside her, I saw my brother Chris standing there, giving a big thumbs-up. I went over and gave him a hug and told him I'd see him when "we" had the baby.

I sat down on a chair outside the surgical suite, since I had to wait until after the cut was made, at which point I would be brought in to witness the baby being pulled out. We had already decided there would be no video of this event, but some discreet black-and-white photos would be okay. I gotta tell you, I was extremely nervous about the procedure. Look, I know Janice Marks has done hundreds of these, but anytime somebody makes a hole in you that wasn't there before, I get nervous. To me, there's no such thing as "minor" surgery!

I really wasn't sure how I was going to react to seeing a baby being pulled out of my wife's belly. I knew that whether it was a C-section or a vaginal birth, I was going to see something happen. Now that the moment was at hand, I didn't know how I was going to handle it. I don't think I'm squeamish, and I really wasn't worried about the syndrome where men who see the birth of their child look at their wife differently, other than the fact that I love her more than ever before for going through all this. I know that if it were up to men to do this, our species would have died out centuries ago.

I was roused out of my reverie when, at about 9:10, Dr. Marks poked her head out the door and said, "Al, we're ready!" I swallowed, picked up my camera, and went inside.

There was my sweetie, head swaddled in a hairnet, and a curtain draped in front of her, preventing us from seeing what was going on. I stroked her cheek, kissed her, and told her that I loved her. Just then, Janice said, "Come on around, Al. Your baby's about to come out." I think I got light-headed at the very prospect of it. Fortunately, one of the delivery room nurses, Meredith, took the camera from me and started snapping shots.

There, coming out of what I knew to be Deborah's belly, although it bore no resemblance to it, was our baby. I heard a sucking noise, and then one of the doctors said, "Ahhh, that's why you didn't want to come out." It seems the umbilical cord was wrapped around the baby's neck a couple of times. Plus it was actually pressing against the cervix. All in all, this would have been a difficult vaginal birth.

As this tiny human being came out, covered

in fluids and blood, all I saw were these lips and a nose and hair and then arms. It was then that Dr. Marks said, "I don't believe it. You called it, Al. Congratulations. You have a beautiful baby daughter!"

A girl. I was right. I knew it. Fannie Flagg, the author and comedienne, wrote a book called *Welcome to the World, Baby Girl.* That's what I felt at that moment. Then I heard the most wonderful sound in the world—her cry. Leila Ruth Roker was letting us know she had arrived, at 9:17 A.M. on Tuesday, November 17, 1998. No meek, namby-pamby delivery for her. A full production number.

They cleaned her off and it was time to cut the umbilical cord. Again, a big swallow, and I walked over to Meredith and Dr. Marks hovering over Leila. One of them clamped the cord, showed me where to cut, and SNIP! It was done. Then it was time for the APGAR test, in which they check response, appearance, and health. Out of 8, Leila scored an 8. All right!

A little goop in her eyes to prevent infection and then they wrapped her up like a baby burrito to show to Mom. When Deborah saw her face, she burst into tears, which in turn started my waterworks. I don't think I've ever felt anything quite like that. Here were a mother and her daughter and I love them both so much. I couldn't wait for Courtney to come to the hospital so I could have all my women together.

Leila was placed in my arms and our new pal Meredith took us back to the LDR Room to wait while they stitched Deborah back up and she recovered from the anesthesia. I sat in the room, holding this tiny bundle. Her eyes were already open and alert. She was looking into my eyes, and I into hers. I got lost in those eyes. Time seemed to vanish, the room disappeared. Afterward, everyone who would visit us would comment on Leila's eyes and how alert she was.

After about twenty minutes, I started making phone calls. My parents, Courtney, Deborah's folks, my sister, her sister. It's still a blur. And more than eighteen months later, I still can't believe I helped create something this beautiful, this wonderful. It wasn't until Leila was eight months old, when my mother was going through some family records, that she discovered something very poignant, eerie, and otherworldly. My baby is named after my maternal grandmother, Leila Smith. Leila Smith died on November 17, 1974. Leila Ruth Roker was born twenty-four years later, on November 17, 1998. I think my grandmother would have liked that. Grandma Smith was a loving, warm woman who loved life. Her great-granddaughter has brought love and warmth into our lives. The acorn didn't fall far from that tree.

SPECIAL DELIVERY, PART 2

After Leila was born, it struck me that the month of November is very special indeed when it comes to me and my babies.

Courtney's mother and my now ex-wife, Alice Bell, and I were married in 1985. For two years after that, we had been trying to have a baby. Alice was a loving mom who already had a fifteen-year-old son, Gregory, when we got married. Before we even became hitched, we had talked about what we would do in the eventuality that we couldn't get pregnant. The options were infertility treatments or adoption. Alice didn't want to go through the infertility stuff, so that left adoption.

A little background on my feelings about adoption. I am the oldest of three boys and three girls. As I mentioned, three of us are biological and three of us are adopted or foster kids. I was the firstborn, but premature. In fact, I only weighed 4 pounds, 10 ounces when I came down the chute a month and a half early. My mom was destined to have difficult pregnancies. She would lose her next child two weeks after birth. My sister Alisa had pneumonia; my brother Chris had his umbilical cord wrapped around his neck several times, causing an emergency during his delivery.

In between these births, my folks decided

to take in foster kids, eventually adopting one and rearing two until they went off to college. So to me, adoption was no big deal. The Rokers are stocky people, low to the ground, built not so much for speed as for stability. Being from the Caribbean, it is a much-desired trait. In a hurricane, we have the edge. Whereas my biological sibs and I are shorter and harder to knock over, my adopted and foster brothers and sisters are leaner, longer, and more lithe.

I hate it when people refer to biological children as being "natural." Folks will say, "So which of your children are natural and which ones are adopted?" Like being adopted makes that child unnatural? They are just as natural as any biological child. When you pick up a child, adopted or not, and hold that baby to your chest and feel that love coming back at you, there's no difference between a biological link or not. It is just there.

So Alice and I decided to adopt. We knew that it might be a long and arduous process, but we felt it was worth it, and I wanted to share my life with an infant, a human being from the ground up. Gregory, while he was a great kid, was part and parcel of Alice and her family and his own father. I wanted to start from scratch with a baby. Boy, girl, didn't matter.

At first, we started with private adoption agencies. There are a number in the New York metro area, and all are well respected and aboveboard. But the way a lot of them work is, they match a couple up with a woman who is pregnant and who, for whatever reason, doesn't want to keep the baby. An agreement is reached and the prospective parents agree to pay for the birth mother's expenses, plus a fee to the agency. These costs can reach $15,000 or more. I'm happy that it works for people. I really am. But it felt to us like we were buying a baby. It just didn't sit well.

Here's how we felt: There were too many minority children in the public sector waiting to be adopted for us to go through a private agency. There were children out there, and it was up to all of us to bring these children into a loving home if we could. We could, and so we decided to look at the Westchester County Department of Children's Services.

In August 1987, we went to the office of Children's Services in White Plains to meet with a caseworker and find out what we had to do. In New York State, there is a several-step process to adopt a child. First, you have to pass muster via a series of interviews and background checks to make sure you're not a criminal or have any history of abuse. You also have to take a four-week course on foster parenting, because once you get a child, you are a foster parent for six months and then the adoption becomes official in the judges' chambers at Family Court.

Our caseworker was a woman named Mrs. Mary Place. I've changed her name and the names of everyone involved with Courtney's adoption. Some folks might be able to piece together where we were and who we dealt with and figure out Courtney's parentage. Until Courtney wants to do that, I don't want it to happen. Even though Alice and I are no longer married, we both agree that if and when Courtney wants to track down her biological parents, we'll help her.

Anyway, Mrs. Place had been working in the system for more than twenty years. She cared about the children who were in her charge. She worked hard with us. And we worked hard, too. When we were told we needed medical exams, we got them the next day and FedExed the results. Told we would need six personal and business references, we divvied them up and went to each person and stood there while they wrote out the references, took 'em, typed 'em up, brought 'em back to the person to sign 'em, and FedExed 'em back to Mary.

Monday, September 7, 1987, we started our foster parenting classes, but we knew that there were very few, if any, African-American babies who were available for adoption. Each week when we came in for class, we would look in the Blue Book, a folder that held the pictures and descriptions of every child in the New York State Child Welfare System. Each week, the same pictures greeted us. All the children were either too old or were "legally at risk." That meant that either one or both parents had not signed away their parental rights to that child and could petition the court to get their baby back. I could not go through that. I had gone through it seventeen years earlier.

My parents had taken in an infant boy named Frankie as a foster child. His parents, who were from Guyana, had given him up temporarily, and the caseworker at Angel Guardian Home, where my other brothers and sisters came from, called my folks to ask them if they had room for one more. He was about two months old when he arrived, and like my other sibs, he was staying with us for a long, long time. None of my other brothers' or sisters' parents had come back for them, so we figured Frankie was with us forever. But six years later, I came home from school and my mother was sobbing. The last time I had seen her cry like that was when my brother Adam died, some ten years earlier.

It turned out that Frankie's parents wanted him back. That week. They were going to take him back to Guyana. It was like a punch in the gut that wouldn't go away. It was then that I learned what "foster care" really meant. These kids could be taken away at any time and there was nothing we could do about it. I still get upset thinking about this little guy who was part of our lives for six years and then was ripped away from us. Just like that.

I would never go through something like that again. So, I would only consider babies who were not "at risk." Then, on October 28, 1987, while we were at the office for our individual personal interviews, I was flipping through the Blue Book, seeing the same faces, when suddenly a new little face was staring at me. I got lost in those big brown eyes and smiling face. I sat bolt upright. This child was mine. I could feel it. A perfect little girl, bald as an eagle, smiling brightly, looking up and off at the future. Our future. I could barely contain myself. I called the number in the book to inquire. I gave her case number and the operator on the other end said, "Ohhh. That one. We've gotten a lot of calls about her." My heart sank. What an idiot! Gee, there's more than one copy of the book? Duhhhh.

When Alice came out of her interview, I showed her the book. It was love at first sight. Mary said she would find out where this little one was located and try to contact the case-worker in charge. We waited outside her office while she made the calls. Thirty minutes later, she came out of her office very excited. "Here's the story," she said breathlessly. "Her name is Gail and she is not at risk. The mother wants to go on with her life and go to college, but wants to make sure this baby is taken care of by a good family. Both she and the father have waived their parental rights." At this point, Alice and I were both getting pretty jazzed. I started saying some silent prayers, hoping against hope that this would, in fact, be my baby.

As it happened, the foster family that was taking care of this baby was white. They had been a foster-care family in this county for more than ten years. For the first time, they wanted to adopt a baby—this baby. As I came to know firsthand, this was a baby you couldn't help but fall in love with as soon as you met her.

I'm not one of those who feel that a white family can't adequately raise a black child. I know there are those who disagree, but I would much prefer to have a kid raised in a stable, loving environment and find out about his heritage along the way than be shuttled from one foster home to the next. He already knows he's black; he should also know what it's like to be in a stable, nurturing, caring home.

That said, we wanted this baby. Hey, these people already had kids of their own. I know this sounds selfish, but you got yours, lemme get mine. Mary suggested that we put together a book of photos, an essay, and some background about ourselves to accompany the official application and information that would be needed for the transfer of this beautiful baby to us as foster parents.

We went home and stayed up all night, culling photos from albums, writing an essay, and putting it all together in a book to be FedExed to this woman upstate, hoping that she would see us as a loving, caring family, people who would be perfect for her. Granted, her dad would not be the most physically attractive guy, and he had a penchant for animated cartoons that went beyond the norm for an adult, but these are attributes that could be overlooked, or at least not mentioned until after she was in our home.

The next day, I shipped the package out, and our caseworker did the same with her official version of our life. It was Thursday, November 5, 1987. It was one of the longest nights of my life. We were on pins and needles, couldn't sleep, wondering whether she would come into our life or this would be a tremendous disappointment. We talked about names that night. Around 3 A.M., we were stuck on Courtney, Samantha, or Melissa. We ruled out Samantha—who wanted to name their kid after a witch on a TV sitcom? We finally decided to name her Courtney Melissa Roker if we were given this amazing gift.

At the time, I was doing local news on the NBC flagship station in New York City, WNBC. The week was dragging because we hadn't heard anything from either our caseworker or the worker upstate. On Wednesday, just after finishing the six o'clock news, my news producer's voice came over the overhead speaker in the studio: "Al, you have a phone call from Alice here in the control room."

Uh-oh, I thought, this can't be good news. I walked into the control room with a sense of dread. My producer handed me the phone.

"What's wrong, Alice?" I asked. "I just thought you'd like to hear this," she answered. I could hear her put the phone down and punch the answering machine. Suddenly, a scratchy, tinny voice came out of the answering machine speaker, transmitted through the phone. I will never, ever forget that moment or those words as long as I live. "Mr. and Mrs. Roker, this is Kathy Hessert from Child Welfare in Such-and-Such County. If you want her, Gail is yours. We'd really appreciate it if you could come to pick her up Monday, since she is bonding with her foster family and we'd like to get her placed as soon as possible."

I remember screaming and jumping up and down right there in the control room. Suddenly, I realized that everyone was looking at me, so I told Alice how happy I was and that I would call her right back as soon as I got to my office. I then explained to my coworkers what had happened and how I was going to be a daddy. Hugs and kisses abounded. Of course, I got a sore face because a lot of these guys hadn't shaved.

That night we were giddy with excitement and anticipation, and in the middle of it all, it hit us. We're going to pick up a baby, and we don't have any baby stuff! Yikes! Whereas most people have several months and a couple of baby showers as preparation, we had exactly four days to outfit a nursery, prepare a layette, and get bottles, car seats, diapers, and so on and so on... It was all pretty overwhelming. We figured we'd have some notice, like a month or two.

The next morning we called Ms. Hessert and told her we would be there first thing Monday morning.

I was anticipating being able to take a week or two off once the baby arrived. But this was November, and while for most people that's no big deal, for a television newsperson, it's a problem. Why? Because November is one of the sweeps months, a period when the ratings are used to determine advertising rates for television stations across the country.

Getting off during the sweeps is impossible. You have to be dead or dying, and even then you need a note from your doctor.

I knew I couldn't take two weeks off, but I figured I could at least grab a week to go get my child and settle in with her. So I went in to see my news director, a guy named John Lane. Well, I was a little surprised when I was told I couldn't take any time off to go get my Courtney. "We're in sweeps and that's that. You cannot take time off!" "But, John," I argued, "if my wife were *having* the baby, you would let me off." He nodded his head in agreement. "Because we're *getting* the baby, I can't have time off?" "That's right," he said.

So basically, we're having a conversation worthy of a *Seinfeld* episode. "John, that's not going to work. I am going to drive on Monday to pick up my five-month-old daughter. I'm leaving on Monday, and I will be back on Thursday. And if you want to fire me, or try to discipline me, that's fine, but you'll have to explain to the gossip columns in the papers why I was punished for adopting a baby." He and I sat there staring each other down. Finally he said, "Make sure you're back here on Thursday." As I left, I replied in as sarcastic a tone as possible, "And thanks for making this such a family-friendly place to work!"

It was now Saturday. This was where the fun began. We had two days to outfit a nursery and a layette. We tore through Macy's, Sears, and Saks, buying up everything we could in

6-to-12-month sizes. We rampaged through Kids "R" Us, snatching up onesies, bottles, bibs, and Pampers. We raced through a juvenile-furniture store, picking up a crib, a dresser, and a rocker. When we finished with the order, Alice asked the manager if he could deliver it on Sunday. "What's your hurry, folks?" he asked. "Well, the baby's coming on Monday!" The man looked at Alice's flat stomach and then looked at us with a puzzled look on his face. "No offense, but when are you due, ma'am?" "No, no," I explained, "we're not pregnant, we're adopting a baby and just found out that we get to pick her up on Monday." "Ohhhh," he replied, still not convinced, but he agreed to make delivery the next day.

Sunday, we split up. Alice went out to get more baby stuff, and I stayed home to await the deliveries and start setting up the nursery. Alice's son, Greg, had been going to college. In fact, he was going to my alma mater, Oswego State University, in upstate New York. His room had been moved to the base-ment where he could put up as many posters with scantily clad cuties hawking beer, car parts, or liquor as he wanted.

So where once the heavy beat of Rapmaster Flash, the Fresh Prince, and Aerosmith emanated, the tunes of Raffi, *Sesame Street,* and Sharon, Lois & Bram would be heard. After the furniture was delivered, I just stood in the middle of the room. In only forty-eight hours, there would be a baby in that crib. It was as frightening as it was exciting.

As the furniture delivery guys came in and out of the house, our dog, Nikki, a retriever-setter mix, padded around, looking quite confused about everything that was going on. I could tell she sensed something was happening, but she couldn't tell what. We hadn't even had time to try to acclimatize her to the fact that she would no longer be the baby in the house. Pet experts tell you to introduce the dog to a doll and to the surroundings the baby will be living in. In our case, it all happened too quickly. We were just going to have to hope for the best and maybe bribe Nikki with Milk-Bones or rawhide chew toys.

Eventually, Alice came home with bag after bag of clothing, layette stuff, and bedding for our little girl. As she brought out each tiny outfit, I felt more and more attached to this little person whom I hadn't even met. She was going to have such an impact on our lives, and we on hers. As Alice put the stuff away, a phone call came in that had the potential to shatter this idyllic setting.

Our caseworker was calling. It seemed the foster family who was caring for Courtney did *not* want to give her up and might not show up with her on Monday at the appointed time. In fact, there was a possibility they might take the Welfare Department to court and try to hold things up.

Great.

So we went to bed that night, not knowing what was going to happen the next day. I had the car all packed and ready to go. We had a long drive ahead of us, including a stopover in Oswego to pick up Greg so he would be there to meet his sister when we did. The last thing I did was to put the infant seat in the back. With any luck, this time tomorrow, there would be a baby filling that seat.

Monday, November 9, 1987, was a cloudy day. And to make matters worse, there was a forecast for a major snowstorm the next day, just when we would be driving back with Courtney. I couldn't worry about that now. And, heck, you know these TV weather people. They're never right.

The ride up was pretty uneventful. We stopped a couple of times to get gas and go to the "potty"— we were already talking like parents with a baby. The unspoken thought that hung between the two of us was, What if that couple doesn't show up with Courtney? What would happen? Would the state troopers show up at their home? "All right! Release the baby and come out with your hands up!" I didn't see that coming to pass, but it could end up in a showdown.

We pulled into Oswego and grabbed Greg from his dorm. I think the baby meant a lot to Alice on a couple of levels. She wanted to share raising a child with me. And second, her first baby, Greg, had gone off to college just that September. I remember how she cried when we pulled away from his dorm that day. One baby was all grown up. Now here she was picking up her first baby, on the way to get her second baby.

I was happy to stop for Greg in Oswego, having graduated from that fine institution of higher learning back in 1976. We stopped for lunch at a place that is, in some small part, responsible for the manly physique I enjoy today. The Oswego Sub Shop is one of the best in the country. Many a night the delivery guy from the Oswego Sub Shop would make a stop at my dorm bearing two roast beef subs with mayo. In the interest of a balanced diet, I would have them add lettuce and tomato. After my gastronomic trip down memory lane, we continued our journey west, toward our baby.

I think we got quieter as we got closer to the city where we would get Courtney. I remember when my parents came home each time with my two sisters and brother from the Angel Guardian Home. There was such anticipation and excitement, but I never thought about it from my parents' point of view. What did it mean to them? Why did they do it? To this day, I've never asked my mom and dad why they decided to open their home to three infants. It's not as if they couldn't have their own children. Maybe it's because they couldn't have enough of them on their own. Both my folks have extremely big hearts. My siblings have inherited that trait, while I also got the big butt from my father's side of the family.

An hour later we were in the town, pulling up to the county office building. I can't remember ever feeling such apprehension and nervousness. We had no idea what to expect. We met Ms. Hessert just outside her office, and the smile on her face told me that our fears were unfounded. I knew there was a little girl waiting to meet her new family.

We were shown into a conference room and sat around a table as if we were going to have some sort of meeting, which I guess we were, in a way—one of the most important meetings of my life. The door opened, and in walked Ms. Hessert holding this little bundle in a pink crocheted outfit. Large brown eyes took in the room, and the people in it. I started to cry. My daughter. She was so beautiful. I couldn't believe how beautiful she was.

We rushed up to meet her, and Alice took her from the caseworker's arms. Understandably, this five-month-old looked a little bewildered and did what five-month-olds do in situations such as these: she started to cry. I mean, she let loose with a wail that shattered glass and had volunteer firemen in two neighboring counties running.

After a while, she quieted down and we all took turns holding her. Ms. Hessert filled us in on what had happened before we got there. It seems that Courtney's foster family did show up, and did relinquish her. There were a lot of tears, but they wanted what was best for her.

Besides bringing Courtney, they brought something almost as precious: a collection of pictures, letters, and other items they had collected during the five months Courtney was in their lives. There was a diary of the time she spent with them—their thoughts and feelings, Courtney's likes and dislikes, her behavior, her moods, her very essence for her first five months on Earth. It was very touching.

These were obviously extremely loving folks, and Courtney would have been a lucky girl to have them as her adoptive parents. I hope the gaping hole that Courtney left was filled by some other little boy or girl. I know from experience how painful it is. How you never forget that child. You always wonder if that kid is doing okay. How did that baby turn out? So far, she's turned out fine. She is everything anyone could ever want in a daughter.

There were papers to sign, and hugs and kisses from all the social workers who had come to know Courtney. Finally, it was time to go. We strapped our little bundle into her seat and away we went, first dropping Greg back at school, then checking into a motel. We had called ahead and requested a crib. After getting settled, the reality of it all hit us. We had a baby. And not just any baby, but the most beautiful baby girl in the world...who was crying...a lot!

I wondered what was going through her mind. Did she miss the family she had been with? Was she trying to figure out who we were? What about these strange surroundings she found herself in? But those questions, if they were rattling around in her bitty brain, didn't seem to stop her from eating. She possessed a very good appetite; Courtney ate what her foster family said she would. Cereal and fruit all disappeared into that little mouth. Quite frankly, I was happy she was eating, because it seemed that if her mouth didn't have food in it, it was open, and very loud noises would come out of it. She was known at the agency as "the crabby one." Now I knew why. Eventually, after dinner, several diaper changes, and a mile or two of walking the floor and rocking her, Courtney finally dropped off to sleep.

I went to bed that night exhausted yet happier, I think, than I had ever been in my life. After an hour of lying awake in bed, listening to a couple next door either trying to make a baby or doing aerobics, I couldn't sleep. I found myself standing next to her crib, watching her sleep. It was a moment I always cherish. My little girl.

The next day we got up early, determined to beat the storm that was forecast. All packed and ready to go, we took off at 8 A.M. An hour south of Oswego, the snow started. We drove through snow, sleet, and ice for the next eight hours, almost twice the time it took us to go pick up Courtney. Alice sat in the backseat with this most precious cargo. I don't think I could have been more nervous. I kept thinking, God wouldn't let us get this far for something to happen to us, would he?

From time to time, I glanced up at the rearview mirror, almost as if to reconfirm there was a baby back there. From time to time, she would let me know. If it wasn't by an audible sound that would make the Emergency Broadcast System alert sound like a whistle in the wind, Courtney made her presence known via her diaper. She could produce a scent that wasn't exactly jasmine wafting over the Holy River. Have you ever tried to change a baby in the backseat of a car during a snowstorm? Take it from me, it ain't easy.

We finally arrived at home, in Westchester County, at 6 P.M. I think my hands were permanently gnarled from gripping the steering wheel so hard, but we were home. Home with a beautiful baby girl with a smile that still illuminates my life. She still lives in Westchester, while I live in New York City, since her mom and I are no longer married. But her mother helped me raise a smart, kind, wonderful daughter. And for that I will be forever grateful.

Courtney settled into her new surroundings without much fanfare. It was as if she had been with us from birth. The only person who seemed a bit put out by the whole thing was our dog, Nikki. She had been used to being the baby and now this interloper had shown up, hogging all the attention.

But even Nikki fell in love with Courtney after the first week, sleeping under her crib, guarding her tenaciously. The only time Nikki vacated her post was if Courtney had a particularly potent diaper. When I saw Nikki lying in the hallway outside Courtney's room, I entered with trepidation.

It was hard to believe that with Leila's arrival I would be dealing with another baby in the month of November. Even harder to believe is that Courtney is past Raffi and *Sesame Street* and all the trappings of childhood as she travels into teenhood. I didn't think I was ready, but then again, who is?

FATHER'S DAY

DON'T MAKE ME STOP THIS CAR!

We all swear that we will not become our parents. I have realized that this is a futile attempt at trying to thwart the inevitable. We have the genetic code built into us that guarantees we will, in fact, become our parents. You can't avoid it. Save the money you'd spend on therapy and get a good home theater with a DVD player.

This isn't exactly a bad thing, mind you. My dad, Al Roker Sr., is a really good guy. I think the world of him. If anything, I think part of any flaws I have may come from my feelings that I will never be as good a father as my dad is, if for no other reason than the fact that he and my mom have been together for forty-seven years. He gave me and my five sibs something money can't buy: a loving home with two parents. It's something that I can't give Courtney because of my divorce. And don't think it isn't something that weighs on me whenever I go to one of her recitals or plays or every time I say good night to her over the phone when she's in her house and I'm in mine.

I had always sworn to myself that when I became a father, I would be a cool dad. I wouldn't use those tired old sayings that have been passed on from generation to generation. You know the ones. "When I was your age, I knew the value of a dollar." ("They had folding money back then, Dad?") Or how about when you screwed up and apologized, your old man came back with, "Well, 'sorry' didn't put out the garbage, did it? 'Sorry' doesn't walk the dog. 'Sorry' won't do your homework." I GET IT!!!!

Up till now I had avoided using those dad-isms. But there was one that made me realize I had taken the first step in becoming my father the minute it crossed my lips. I had been driving Courtney and two of her cousins down to Six Flags Great Adventure in central New Jersey. Traffic was bad, and the kids were worse. We were all trapped in the Explorer and the longer the drive took, the worse these kids became. I begged, pleaded, and cajoled, trying to get them calmed down. Finally, those six little words came out involuntarily, the ones I had heard my father use with us some thirty years ago.

DON'T MAKE ME STOP THIS CAR!

When my father would say it, it struck fear into the entire brood. Why? Because we believed my father *would* stop the car. We didn't want to find out what would happen if he *did* stop the car. Would he leave us on the side of the road? Would he drop us off one by one? Our minds boggled at the possibilities.

You want to talk about road rage? Put six screaming kids and a nagging wife in a car with a man who had already spent eight hours driving hostile New Yorkers in a bus and see what you get. My father was a saint to put up with us.

Anyway, that statement would quiet us down for a period of ten to twenty minutes, depending on how loudly he said it. But you put six kids in a 1967 Ford Country Squire station wagon, and all hell is gonna break loose eventually. Perhaps you're too young to remember the Country Squire station wagon. It was the '60s version of the minivan. This thing was the size of a boat with fake wood trim on the sides.

It had a flip-up seat in the back cargo area. My brother Andrew and I would fight for those seats back there. Who knew that it was probably a death zone? They should've just painted a bull's-eye on the tailgate and called it a day. One good rear impact and it would've been kiddie pâté.

After getting us to pipe down for a while, we would get nuts again. "You're on my side." "No, I'm not." "Are too." "Am not." "Mom, he's looking at me funny." "Am not."

"Are too." Finally, my father would explode. "THAT'S IT! I DON'T CARE WHO DID WHAT. I'M REACHIN' BACK THERE AND I'M HITTIN' SOMEBODY!!!" Now we would all try to avoid this arm waving around the backseat like the tentacle of some giant sea monster. We would press ourselves against the window kind of like precursors to those suction-cup Garfields that grace minivans all across America.

The car would be weaving back and forth all over the road, with my mother screaming in the front seat. My father, frustrated that he couldn't mete out some driver justice, developed a maneuver that took care of the problem. The first left turn he could make, he'd take it...hard. We would come sliding across the faux leather seats and he could use our momentum against us. WHAM!! Lemme tell ya, that quieted us down.

Those six little words worked for my father because we were afraid. Courtney has never been really spanked. She doesn't have the fear you and I had of our fathers.

Courtney couldn't relate to any of this. The most she's ever gotten was a swat on her Pampers-padded bottom if she didn't listen, and only after repeated time-outs failed to produce the desired result. Come to think of it, the only "time-out" we got was if my dad couldn't find the belt. Lest I give the impression that mine was a childhood filled with nonstop spankings, nothing could be further from the truth. Because we were afraid of the belt, it was a deterrent to crime.

When I look back, there were only two or three times I really got spanked. Spanking meant the use of a belt or a wooden spoon or the flat of a hand. Each time, I have to say, I really deserved it. And after that, the mere threat of the belt was enough to keep me on the straight and narrow. My dad could get the belt off in one fluid motion and make a sound with it not unlike that of Indiana Jones's whip cracking. If we got out of hand at the dinner table, he would push back, get up, and whip off the belt. We'd hear that cracking sound and stop doing whatever we were doing and wet our pants.

On the rare occasion when the belt would actually make contact, it wasn't the sting of the belt that was so bothersome. It was that stupid saying he'd preface the spanking with: "This is going to hurt me more than it does you!" Wanna bet? Let's trade places and see if it's true. Of course, we were never crazy enough to say that!

It was a different time. Spanking was okay. It isn't now. And that's a good thing. Recent studies show that spanking doesn't really achieve the behavior parents are hoping for. Where were these people about thirty-five years ago? Could have saved me a lot of trouble and several pairs of wet trousers!

BABY-PROOFING

Once Leila started crawling, we decided it was time to baby-proof the apartment. Americans have become so paranoid about the dangers that lurk in our homes and apartments that it's not enough to install cabinet locks or put gates on the stairs. A whole industry has sprung up. Professional baby-proofers will come to your abode and make sure your most precious of possessions will be as safe as possible.

I hired one of these companies that was recommended by someone Deborah works with. I think I'm in the wrong business. Talk about a growth industry. First, the receptionist told me there would be a monthlong wait. It seems there's a mini baby boom going on, and these baby-proofers are much in demand. Can there be that many lazy parents out there? I thought I was the only one who lacked the time and a power screwdriver to crawl around my apartment attaching cabinet latches.

Second, after telling this women the size of our apartment and the approximate number of cabinets and drawers, Baby-proof Lady gave me an estimate that approached five hundred dollars. YIKES! But let's face it: (A) I knew that my handyman skills approach those of Daniel Day-Lewis in *My Left Foot,* and (B) I didn't want to appear cheap when it came to my baby's safety.

After much begging and a promise of three custom weather forecasts whenever she needed them, I convinced the nice lady that mine was a home of unspeakable horrors: cabinets and drawers that contained radioactive materials, knives, explosives, and farm equipment that could burst forth at any moment. She took pity on me and scheduled an appointment for the following week. She advised that either my wife or I be present, in addition to the babysitter, so they could go over baby safety with us.

Leila was like any other crawling infant. Any place you didn't want her to be, she immediately was drawn to it like a magnet. Open closets, flights of stairs, basement doors, were like honey to a fly. I had gone through this with Courtney, so I knew that babies survive quite nicely. My first daughter was a world-class stair climber. She could make it up the stairs before you could say, "Come away from there."

She was part of that group of children that grew up right in the middle of the "safety age." Baby-proofing came of age as my first girl was coming of age. And as she grew, so did the safety technology. From safe kitchens and bathrooms, she moved on to playgrounds with soft surfaces. As Courtney became more mobile, her generation was the first to really use bicycle helmets and skating protection like helmets, wrist guards, and knee pads.

If you're my age, when we were kids, baby-proofing consisted of putting some rubber bands around the cabinet knobs in the kitchen and a firm "NO," followed by a little smack on the wrist. It is amazing that any of us survived to the age of five. And when you got past the crawling, toddling, falling stage and made it to kid status, there were further hazards from which we were unprotected. Take the playground. Everywhere you looked, there were death traps. Did you have monkey bars at your playground? If you did, you know what I'm talking about. A vertical maze made up of interconnected steel pipes forming squares that rose up about 8 to 10 feet off the ground, anchored to a base of asphalt or cement. I guess the idea was to create a climbing "environment" for children. In theory it was a great idea. In reality, one slip and you went bouncing off metal pipe on your way to the bottom like a human pinball.

Remember the teeter-totter or seesaw? It was the ultimate test of endurance and trust. As you went up in the air, your partner came down to the ground. Once you were suspended up there, you secretly prayed that your so-called friend wouldn't jump and send you plummeting to the ground. Just the thought of hitting the ground with that board between my legs makes me shiver.

Then there's the subject of bicycles and roller skates. Bike helmets? Don't make me laugh. All we had was a baseball cap, a coaster brake, and in case of the need for an emergency stop, our own two feet. Metal, clamp-on roller skates were the rule of the day. A skate key to tighten the skates onto your Keds or PF Flyers was the only tool you had.

Anyway, a baby-proofing guy showed up at the apartment and immediately gave me a ream of child safety information, launching into a spiel about what he was going to do, why he was going to do it, and the time it would take. An apprentice showed up about ten minutes later and for the next three hours, they crawled around on hands and knees, locating potential hazards and fixing them.

Electrical outlet plates were replaced with spring-loaded covers that automatically closed when plugs were removed. Padding for the coffee table, gates for rooms that we didn't want Leila to go into, and straps to bundle electrical cords out of the way were all put in place. The additions that are *still* driving me crazy, yet I know are necessities, are the cabinet and drawer latches. If you have kids, I'm sure you know what I'm talking about: plastic latches that hook onto the catches of a drawer or cabinet and prevent the offending item from opening any more than one or two inches.

Baby-proof Man was a slender guy with thin fingers. So what was an ample amount of space for him to slip a couple of fingers into and release the latch proved to be a tighter fit for yours truly. Now it takes me about three minutes to open the flatware drawer. On the other hand, because it takes so long for me to get the pantry doors open, I lose interest in whatever it was I was going to go in and get to eat. As an indirect result, I'm losing a little weight.

Of course, my little Houdini has figured out the latches to the undersink cabinet in the kitchen, causing me to add several different latches and a combination lock. As with child-proof prescription bottles, the only people who *can't* open them are adults. Whenever you make something to keep a kid out, they will work on it until they can get in. Why do you think all the computer hackers are kids? My daughter has a bright future compromising the security of the Pentagon or the National Security Council.

I'M A DAD, NOT A BABY-SITTER

Here's one of the things that drives me crazy. I am walking with Leila through Central Park on a lovely spring afternoon. My daughter is smiling at me, the birds are chirping, the sun is shining, the trees are budding. Nothing can ruin my day. So I think.

As I'm walking, some woman comes up and smiles, recognizing me, and leans in to take a look at Leila. "She is beautiful," the woman chirps. "Thank you," I reply. Then she comes back with the words that make me nuts. "So, you're baby-sitting this afternoon, eh?"

I take a breath and smile back at her with

my best face on and say, "No, ma'am. I'm not. I'm with my daughter." She smiles back, looks a little perplexed, and moves on. Once again, the ol' double-edged sword comes slicing out of the trees to cut down the dad.

What am I talkin' about? I'm talkin' about the difference in parents. Moms versus dads. Now, think about it. Whenever anybody sees a woman walking with her baby, does anyone come up to her and go, "Say, Miss. That's a beautiful baby you have there. Are you baby-sitting this afternoon?" Nooooooooooooo. They just assume the woman is taking care of her child. Nurturing, loving, caring.

Dad, on the other hand, is a boob, not to be trusted. Hey, we've all seen the countless sitcoms on TV where the father loses the kids, or does something goofy with the kids. In our society, leaving the baby with Daddy is just one step above leaving the child to be raised by wolves or apes. And at least with apes, the kid learns to swing from trees, wear a loincloth, and develop a kick-butt yodel.

I gotta tell you, I, for one, have had it. Dads can, in fact, take care of their children. When a father is with his child, it's not baby-sitting, it's parenting. And he can do it just as well as Mom. Now look, I'm no idiot. Well, a dolt perhaps, but certainly no idiot. There are dads out there who wouldn't know the business end of a diaper even if it came with labels. But there are moms like that, too. That's no reason to tar the rest of us dads with the same dirty diaper.

I know plenty of fathers who do more than take their kids into the backyard for the occasional game of catch. My father was one of them. He showed us how to cook, how to clean, how to be good people. My fondest memories of growing up are the days spent with my dad when he would take me to work with him.

When I was seven years old, my father drove a New York City bus in Brooklyn. His bus depot was the inspiration for the fictional bus depot for the Gotham Bus Company. Its most famous driver? None other than Ralph Kramden, aka Jackie Gleason. When they tore down the depot about ten years ago, the new one was renamed the Jackie Gleason Depot. Sometimes we kids used to call Dad "Ralph" behind his back.

He was respectful of his passengers and they with him. His uniform was always cleaned and pressed, his shoes shined, and his hat sat just so on his head. I loved going to the depot with him. We'd get up around 5 A.M. and drive to "the Barn," as some of the guys called it.

It was a huge open room, the biggest I had ever seen. In the center of the room, ten money-counting machines were constantly going. Drivers would come in from their routes and empty their fare boxes into the counters. The machines would count and bag the money for the men to take to the money room. There was a constant din from the machines. They had a rhythm that was always going in the background.

I loved going for two reasons. I enjoyed the time I spent with Dad, one-on-one, no brothers or sisters to share him with. The other reason was the food. It was a great racket being seven years old and being at the depot with your father.

The depot had a very Damon Runyon–esque feel to it. On one side of the room there were rows of old, scarred wooden tables where the bus drivers ate, filled out forms, or just hung out. No matter what time of the day or night, there would be at least two card games going. I would watch as these men would laugh, swear, and yell at each other. Invariably, some of my dad's pals would walk by and rub my head or chuck me on the shoulder. "So, this is Little Al, huh? Looks just like his dad," they would say. Then the guy would rummage around in his pants pocket and fish out a stick of gum or a roll of Life Savers or a quarter and press it into my hand. Other bus drivers would take you to the vending machines and buy you candy or ice cream. You could clear three or four dollars and end up with enough candy to start a store. After ten or fifteen minutes of kibitzing, shooting the breeze, and catching up on the latest depot gossip (who banged up what bus, who was cashing out for retirement), my dad would lead me back to the locker room and from there to the garage to pick up our bus. The bus drivers' locker room was a mystical place to me. Not having been in a locker room at school yet, this was the closest I had come.

Row upon row of olive green lockers with wooden benches in front of them lined the room. When some of the guys would open those metal doors, what would be taped up on the inside? NAKED WOMEN! *Playboy* pin-ups and calendars adorned these lockers. HUBBA HUBBA. My father would be talking to his buddy, and I'd be trying to sneak a look at the "gallery." The longer my dad talked, the more I got to see. My father always told my mother that I wouldn't be bored on these outings. He was right. And they were educational. Of course, for the longest time, I thought women folded in thirds and had a staple in their navel.

Once my father was dressed in his uniform and I was on the bus with him, I felt so special. My dad would introduce me to his regulars. We'd see them on their way to work and on their way home.

During break time, we'd stop at Goody's Luncheonette in Flatbush to have egg creams and halvah. Dad would buy me two dollars' worth of comic books and I would be in heaven. Then came lunchtime and we'd open up the brown-bag lunch my mother had packed for her two men at work. We would sit in the bus, pulled over to the side of the road, my dad and I, eating and talking about television, the Yankees, school, or whatever came to mind. Just before we'd come off lunch, Dad would sit in the driver's seat, then hoist me up onto his lap. He'd start up the engine, release the brake, and let me steer.

Ever try to steer a bus? Big steering wheel, barely power assisted. It was just you, brawn, and the ability to turn that leviathan. My father's strong, steady hands were on the wheel as well, and looking back on it, we probably traveled only 50 feet, but it could've been 50 miles for all I cared. I got to do something none of my friends did, and I got to do it with my dad.

Today, Courtney comes into work with me on a regular basis. She's long been over the fact that Daddy works at a TV station or at the *Today* show. Long before Take Our Daughters to Work Day, Courtney has been going to the job with her mother, a politician in Westchester County, New York, and with me.

She's grown up around the likes of Matt Lauer, Katie Couric, and Ann Curry. And forget about being around me. No big thing. Her classmates would come down for a field trip to the NBC studios, and Courtney's big request was, "Dad, please don't mention to everyone that I'm your daughter!" It's obvious the embarrassment quotient is very high. God, my father is a...TV weatherman.

I don't know if she gets the same satisfaction I did when I was hanging out with my father. Being behind the wheel of a 20-ton bus is a lot different from sitting in a studio watching your pop gesture at a blank blue wall, as all TV weather people must do. My dad actually did something physical. He drove a bus. Me, I do the weather. I stand in front of a camera. Which is more enjoyable to a kid? Maybe it doesn't matter. Maybe it's enough just to be there. I sure hope so.

BABY GERMS

There is nothing like your first child. You love all your children equally, and you would do anything for all of them. But there slowly but surely is a change in your attitude toward your children. You learn that they are incredibly resilient creatures who are able to thrive in this cold, cruel world quite nicely with a minimum amount of care.

I think about how I was with Courtney. Everything had to be sterilized and kept incredibly clean, and if anything had a whiff of uncleanliness, it was either thrown out, burned, or buried. Say her bottle fell on the floor in our house. That bottle was immediately emptied and placed in the autoclave for sterilization. I actually increased the water temperature of the hot water heater so that no germ could possibly survive our dishwasher or washing machine. Before anybody could touch her, they were sent to the bathroom and told to wash their hands vigorously with antibacterial soap.

Slowly, I relaxed this fanatical devotion to protecting Courtney from the dangers of unseen germs. It came from observing parents who had multiple kids. For example, whereas I kept Courtney's bottle germ-free, I would see other kids drop their bottle and their mother wipe it off and stick it back in the wailing orifice as quickly as possible. Or, I have witnessed a father take a bottle, stick it in his mouth, suck it clean, and then give it back to the infant. I guess this practice is in accordance with the theory that a baby is immune to any germ the parent has.

Seeing this for the first time I was repulsed, but then I thought back to the stuff my mother would do. In the beginning, with each of my brothers and sisters, she would indeed do the boiling and sterilization. But as each of us got stronger and had the necessary immune system to survive the outside world and, what's more important, each other, Mom would get a little more lax about the cleanliness thing. She would use the "bottle in her mouth" technique. Of course, the extension of that is using maternal saliva as an all-purpose cleaning solution.

Think about it. How many times did you have something on your face and your mother would lean over you, lick her fingers, then wipe off the offending smudge? If there was a tissue handy, she might dab that on her tongue, then wipe your face with it. I think it all goes back to the whole feline-woman thing: mommy cats lick their kittens clean after meals. Same concept. Heck, I've done the same thing with Courtney and Leila. Okay, I don't do it anymore with Courtney, but Leila doesn't know any better.

Even now I find myself sucking a bottle that found its way to the floor and sticking it back in Leila's mouth if there's no water present. I still make people wash their hands before touching her or, if there's no water around, I whip out a pocket-size bottle of Purell and squirt 'em. See, she's immune to *my* germs, but not yours.

Unfortunately, it doesn't work the other way around. Baby germs will kick your butt six ways to Sunday. I remember Courtney caught a cold the first week she started at the day care center at the Montessori school in our town. She was over it in about a week. I caught her cold, was out sick for two days, and didn't actually shake the cold for almost three weeks.

My theory is that baby germs are particularly virulent because they have to be stronger to overcome a baby's very powerful immune system. Infants and toddlers are constantly sticking dirty, nasty things in their mouths—shoes, pets, stroller wheels, you name it. If we put half the things in our mouths that they do, we'd be dead in a week.

Babies survive. Why? Because of their germ-fighting system. It's made of strong stuff because babies don't know *not* to put those things in their mouths. Once they learn the dos and don'ts of what's appropriate for the mouth, the system slackens off. Until then, these germs have to be *really* strong to overcome that tough baby immune system. Germs invade;

baby immune system kicks their butts; germs think, I'm finding me someone who's not so tough. Who's available? Mom and Dad!

That's why whenever one of my co-workers who has kids shows up with a cold, I avoid that person like the plague. I sympathize with 'em, but leave me alone. You've got baby germs. And baby, that's tough!

A WHOLE LOT OF FIRSTS

It was a lazy Saturday afternoon. Courtney was in her room with a friend from camp, Deborah was out shopping, and I had Leila in our family room watching a tape of *Sesame Street*. Already hooked on Elmo, but who isn't? At this point, Leila still hadn't learned how to walk yet, but she had developed the fine art of the cruise-crawl. For speed, she would crawl like crazy to get to where she wanted to be. Then she would hoist herself up and start to walk, using a couch or a cabinet to support herself.

This one afternoon, I had walked into the kitchen and heard the familiar sound of her palms slapping the floor and the skuff-skuff-skuff of her shoes against the wood. No matter how much you wash, it seems there are always baby bottles in the sink waiting to be scrubbed and sanitized. I was standing at the sink and she was standing at the fridge when suddenly her feet went out from under her. As if it was in slow motion, I saw my baby's face catch the edge of the fridge's door handle.

She lay there for a second or two silently, then her mouth opened wide and this blood-curdling scream emanated from where just moments earlier laughs and giggles were coming from. I rushed over, scooped her up, and looked at her. Two little points of blood were forming on her lip. Then, as I looked at her still open mouth, I noticed blood on her two front teeth.

Suddenly I saw one tooth up a little farther than the other one. Great. Leila's picture-perfect smile had just been altered. About a minute had passed, and my baby buried her face into my shoulder, snuffling and alternating between crying and trying to smile. "Lemme see dose toofs! Lemme see dose toofs!" I said, trying to make her laugh while attempting to get a better look to see if there was any major damage.

Carrying my girl into the family room, I called

our pediatrician to get his advice. Just then, Deborah walked in and saw Leila. "Hi, Leila! It's Mommy. How's my girl? Have you been crying?" Deborah looked at me quizzically and asked was Leila crying? Man, I was dreading this. Let's face it. No one wants to be the P.O.D. when something happens to your baby. What is P.O.D.? you ask. Parent On Duty. One parent is gone, so the other one is in charge. It's always best, when the absent parent returns, that things are as good as or better than they were before.

While I don't think I was panicking, I will readily admit that I was freaking out a little bit, not so much because of the severity of the boo-boo, but the type of boo-boo. When I was around eight years old, I was not the most coordinated child physically. All right, I was a klutz. Okay, ya happy? You got it out of me. Anyway, I was playing catch with some friends on the playground in front of our apartment house after school when I slipped on the ball I was supposed to catch. Now, most kids would use their hands to break their fall. I used my face. I did a real number on it, but I didn't know how bad it was till my mother got home later that afternoon. The way she tells it, I was sitting at the kitchen table, doing my homework, holding to my head a dishtowel that was soaked in blood. There was a huge scrape down the front of my face from head to chin. When she asked me what happened I was a little hard to understand because I was keeping my tongue over my teeth. Why? I had busted my two front teeth and was using my tongue to cover the nerve, which was hanging out, to keep the air from hitting it. I'll give you a chance to stop shuddering involuntarily. So I have a bad history with dental injuries. And with that in mind, I didn't want Leila to get off on the wrong foot, dentally speaking.

Deborah, on the other hand, was quite calm about the whole thing and seemed to think Leila didn't even need to see our pediatrician. Me, I wanted to play it safe. By now, as far as Leila was concerned, the whole thing had blown over and she was ready to play. Any sniffles had long passed, the tears had been dried, and now was the time for all good strollers to come to the aid of their babies.

The visit to the doctor confirmed what everyone *but* me seemed to know: Leila's tooth was fine. In fact, the only injury as far as I was concerned was to my record. As the P.O.D., I had an enviable record of no major problems on my watch. Now that record is blemished. Luckily, my baby isn't.

It's the moment every parent lives for. No, not when your kids move out. For us that's a long way off. I'm talking about the first unsteady steps one's baby takes.

For Leila, it was about three weeks before her first birthday when Deborah stood her up, then moved back a few paces and held out her arms to Leila. Standing up on her own, Leila grinned at her mommy, then took those steps.

Arms stretched out in front of her, ramrod straight, tottering side to side, legs stiff, she looked like a very cute Baby Frankenstein.

She fell into Deborah's waiting arms. Both of them clapped for the milestone that just occurred. I was at work, preparing for the five o'clock news, when Deborah called to tell me the news. I was excited and jealous. I had missed Leila's first steps. Drat! That evening I was supposed to meet some friends for dinner, but there was no way I was missing the chance to see her the night she first started walking. If I went out, Leila would be asleep by the time I got home, so I made a detour to the apartment and a beeline for my daughter.

But it was not to be that night. My little girl was all walked out. Try as I might to stand her up, she would just drop down into her crawling position and scoot over to her daddy. Oh, well. But the next evening, she was ready and walked for Daddy several times. We even got it on video so that we would be able to save the moment for posterity.

When it came to Courtney's first steps, it just so happened that I was home, cleaning the camcorder, when I focused on her holding on to the coffee table. She was about thirteen months old and I was about to get dressed to head into the city to do the news. While I waited for the baby-sitter to arrive, I pressed the Record button to make sure I hadn't screwed it up and, looking through the viewfinder, I saw Courtney taking those first unsure steps. I didn't want to spook her, so I just kept looking through the camera's viewfinder, with that red dot blinking, indicating that I was actually recording my daughter's wobbly first steps.

I can't tell you how exciting that was. I still remember that feeling to this day. One of those goose-bumpy feelings that stays with you for the rest of your life.

Our biggest concern with Leila was that we'd both miss the moment. With Deborah's travel and my schedule, the odds were that our baby-sitter, Evette, would get to see Leila walk before we did. In fact, we've come to an understanding. If Leila performs some milestone, Evette knows to let us discover it on our own. For all I know, Evette's already seen Leila play the piano, balance the checkbook, and recite the Gettysburg Address. But if she has, she's not letting on. So if you see Leila performing with Riverdance, don't say anything. Let us find out for ourselves.

When Leila was ten months old, we took our first vacation without the children. Courtney had just started seventh grade and was in school. Leila stayed with my parents. We were...alone.

It had been two years since we had gone on a "single" vacation—a vacation where no one was worried about the kids, about bottles, about keeping a preteen from being "booooooooored." It took some getting used to. Heck, it took a lot just to get out the door.

To me, two years seems like such a long time not to have a vacation to ourselves. Then I started thinking about my parents. My folks didn't take a vacation away from the six of us until I was in high school. In our world, a vacation was an outing with the kids. Ours wasn't a world of trips to Paris or the Hamptons or even the Catskills. Ours was a world of packing everybody into that 1967 Ford Country Squire station wagon, hooking up with other family members in similar vehicles, and caravanning upstate to Bear Mountain or Anthony Wayne State Park in Orange County, about an hour and a half north of New York City, or Mohansic State Park in Westchester. To a kid from Queens, these locations were really "upstate." My poor Dad had to listen to the same questions that every father or mother who ever put a child in the backseat has heard: "Are we there yet?" "How much farther?" "Can I go to the bathroom?" I imagine some father was driving the *Mayflower* and his Pilgrim child comes out of the cabin onto the ship's deck and asks in his little English accent, "How much farther, Father?" Or riding across the Oregon Trail on the way to California for the Gold Rush, a pioneer child pokes his or her head out of the covered Conestoga wagon (with real wood trim on the side, unlike the Country Squire wagon) and says, "Say, Pappy, are we there yet?"

The trick was to be on the road early to be able to get to the parking lot first. This way you could get prime parking spaces. The most coveted were the ones closest to the picnic area and swimming pools, thus minimizing the distance everything had to be lugged. My father was usually in charge of logistics. A Gemini rocket was launched with less precision than a picnic planned by my dad.

An exact timetable was called in to each family participating in the drive up to the picnic. Menus were coordinated so that there wasn't a surplus of, say, potato salad or peas and rice. Rendezvous points were mapped out and distributed along with directions. Woe betide the family vehicle that wasn't at its appointed spot at the appointed time along the route. They were left behind and left to fend for themselves. If they missed their checkpoint, odds were they would be doomed to an inferior spot in a distant parking lot.

Once we did get there, it was a wonderful time, full of simple pleasures and great moments: softball and volleyball with aunts and uncles; swimming with brothers, sisters, and cousins; and eating till you felt like you were going to burst.

My mother was a fanatic about food spoiling. She would mentally make a note of what time something was taken out of any given Coleman cooler and set out on a picnic table. My mom could hear bacteria growing. She could see microorganisms perched on top of the macaroni salad waiting to attack her children. To this day, I set a stopwatch to food left outside the refrigerator. It's a trait that I'm quite proud of and I feel holds me in good stead in a world gone mad as far as exotic strains of bacteria are concerned.

And the problem with swimming was the dreaded "twenty minute" rule. All of us were told we couldn't go swimming for twenty minutes after we ate. I was never quite sure what the consequences of going swimming less than twenty minutes after you ate were. We had heard vague rumors of children sinking to the bottom of the pool, then their ham and cheese–laden stomachs would fill with a mysterious gas, expand ten times natural size, and sending them hurtling up from the depths of the pool, causing "the bends" and certain death.

Because of the haze surrounding the consequences of the "twenty minute" rule, on any given weekend you could see hundreds of children lined up at the water's edge, calling over to their mothers, "How much longer?" The parents, immersed in card games, eating, or reading, called out random times. They stretched the "twenty minute" rule out to about an hour, knowing this was the only peace they'd get during the trip, the rest of the time being spent watching the kids, getting food for the kids, packing up, and answering the infamous question on the way back.

The irony of all this was that some twenty years later, I moved waaaaaay upstate to a town very close to Mohansic State Park. My daily commute to Manhattan was almost an hour. But when I was ten years old, it felt like the once-a-year trip took forever.

So I feel like a world-class whiner when I talk about not having had a vacation with my wife for two years. As the day approached to leave for our trip to Paris and Venice, we started to get more apprehensive about leaving Leila. I wasn't worried about leaving her with my parents. They know all about raising kids—their own and thirteen grandchildren.

I remember the first time I was going to be leaving Courtney. Her mother and I were going to Nassau in the Bahamas. She was just about a year old, and had come down with a mild cold. We showed up at my parents' door with the prescriptions Courtney's pediatrician had given us and every over-the-counter medicine you could think of. I started to tick off the list of medicines and procedures that Courtney would need when my mother held up her hand. "Hold on there, buster," my mom exclaimed. "We had six children. Last time I checked, you were all still alive. Your father and I know what to do. Get out of here and go have a good time."

And lo and behold, my daughter survived and thrived under her grandparents' care. Courtney got to do what a lot of children unfortunately don't get to do much: spend time with her grandparents. We are so spread out now as a society that we live great distances from our parents, grandparents, and siblings.

So, with that in mind, we arrived at my parents' doorstep with Leila in tow. These days, you don't just show up with a baby and a diaper bag. Oh, no, there is so much more.

Portable playpen/crib, Sassy seat, high chair, toys, diapers, Desitin, Vaseline, formula, bottles, dishes, spoons, baby food, and favorite books, bears, and dolls.

My father looked at the mound of Leila stuff sitting in the middle of the living room and said, "I just want to be sure. You guys are going away for just a week, right?" I replied meekly, "Well, I just wanted to make sure you guys had enough stuff." "Guess what? They do have stores out here in Queens. I see other grandparents in Shop Rite buying things for their grandchildren," he answered.

After spending an hour with my folks, it was time for us to head to the airport. I hugged my baby and kissed her good-bye, and Deborah did the same. We waved to our daughter standing in the doorway with Nana and Pop-Pop and drove to the airport. Later my father told me that he and my mom both were certain we would call from the airport to check on Leila. We didn't let them down.

I think there is a biological thing going on here. While dads tend to miss their baby, moms are more likely to demand that the pilot turn the plane around and head back to the airport so that they can get one more hug from their child. I convinced Deborah that we should not call from the plane, that we should probably allow my folks at least a six-hour period when they didn't hear from us.

While I was quite content to watch *The Matrix* and *Austin Powers*, Deborah stared out the airplane window, thinking about our little Leila and whether she was sleeping soundly or giving her grandparents fits. Whereas I was pretty pleased with my meal, Deborah was worried that Leila might not have eaten enough of hers.

We eventually fell asleep on the overnight trip to Paris and finally arrived at our hotel. Up in the room, as I was tipping the bellboy, I could hear Deborah dialing the phone. Fortunately, she remembered that New York is six hours behind Paris and we would be calling my parents at 1 A.M. their time. We would have to wait another six hours before we could attempt a call to see how Leila was. Twelve hours is a long time to be out of contact with your child if it's never happened before.

After a little therapeutic shopping for Deborah, we got back to the hotel and dialed the number. My father picked up the phone and said, "Hello, you two. Your daughter's fine." Deborah started laughing and asked how our precious one was. They proceeded to tell us how good she was, how easily she ate, and what a dream she was to put to sleep. In other words, she barely knew we were gone.

On the one hand, I was ecstatic to hear that Leila's first night with my folks, as good as they are, went without a hitch. A baby doesn't always adapt to new surroundings right away. On the other hand, I guess there was a part of me that wanted to hear she was a little fussy, indicating that she missed Mommy and Daddy. My mother and father went on and on about how she went to sleep right on schedule, and my mother twisted the knife a little by voicing my deepest fear. "This one doesn't seem to be missing anybody," she cooed.

Our pattern for the rest of the trip was to make a call in the morning, East Coast time, and one in the late afternoon. As each day went on, we became more and more relaxed about being away from Leila and started enjoying ourselves more and more. There would be moments of guilt about being away from her, but I'd take a deep breath, let it out slowly, and those moments would pass.

A week later, we were back home. Driving directly from the airport to my folks' house, we awakened our little Sleeping Beauty and whisked her home. I cannot tell you how good it is to know that you can pick up and go, safe in the knowledge that the people who loved you and raised you will be there for your child. We both know that we are extremely fortunate. Deborah's folks live in Georgia, so it's not like we can just drop Leila off on the way to the airport. And just think, before we know it, Leila will be begging us to drop her off at Nana and Pop-Pop's—even if we're not going away on a trip.

WE ARE FAMILY

As I'm driving my family in our spiffy minivan/sport utility/station wagon/assault vehicle, I'm struck by an interesting thought. I am stuck between Huggies and hormones. Between Barney and Brandy.

Kids ten and under are dependent on you for the basic necessities of life, and they know it. Sustenance, clothing, shelter, and video games. Chances are you're still bigger than they are. Control is still within your grasp. Enjoy it.

I know from whence I speak. You see, I have sitting in the backseat of this vehicle an eighteen-month-old and in the very backseat of the truck a (gulp) freshly minted teenager. Leila Ruth is eighteen months old, while Courtney is thirteen years old. I am right in the middle of all this. Raging hormones and excessive exposure to MTV have rendered my once precious baby into a sullen know-it-all who barely tolerates me.

What was my interesting thought? Just that family history is repeating itself. My father and mother, Al and Isabel Roker, had a big spread between their oldest and youngest as well. I am the oldest of the six Roker siblings. My brother Chris is seventeen years younger. Courtney is eleven years older than Leila. A nice symmetry there, but for one little thing. The difference? My dad was thirty-eight and my mom was thirty-six when they had their last child. I am almost forty-six years old with a toddler and a thirteen-year-old.

I was thirty-two when Courtney arrived. She's thirteen now. Hey, that's not so bad. I've got plenty of guy friends who are in their mid-forties with teenagers. The problem is, I've got plenty of guy friends in their mid-forties who have spankin', brand-new babies. You do the math. Leila's almost two. When she's ten, I'm fifty-four. When she's twenty, I'm sixty-four. When she's thirty...well, you get the idea. It's a little depressing. You think I'm kidding?

Recently, I'm shopping at the grocery store and some little old lady walked up to me and said, "Oh, what a beautiful little girl. Is this your first grandchild?" I was stunned! *Grandchild?* "This is my daughter, ma'am! Do I look old to you? Do I look like I'm *your* age? *Huh? Huh?*" It was then that I noticed she was cowering behind a display of canned artichokes and that a security guard was headed in our direction. I mumbled something about my medication being adjusted and hurried out of the store.

Leila Ruth's arrival has made me confront the basic fact that I'm getting older. I realize, when I get down on the floor with her, it's taking me a little longer to get up. Actually, a lot longer to get up. In fact, I just lie on the floor and let her find the little bags of Cheerios I have stashed in various pockets. Sort of Daddy as Treasure Island. Playing "horsie" makes

149

Daddy wish they would take Ol' Paint to the glue factory and call it a day. I look forward to playing hide 'n' seek so I can find a reall-llly good hiding spot and take a nap.

With Courtney, I have a whole different set of issues. Music, schoolwork, getting her into a convent until she's thirty. Things like that. Everything I wreaked upon my parents as a teenager is being revisited upon me as an adult. Again, the car seems to be a focal point of our differences. Like any healthy, red-blooded, American teen, Courtney enjoys listening to the radio. In our area that would be Z-100, a station that plays a mix of rock, rap, R & B, and pop. Over and over and over again. And if Courtney doesn't hear a song on that station that hasn't been played within the last, say, ten minutes, she's got the radio programmed to a variety of stations that will play her music.

When I was a teenager, my dad had a simple rule. "He who steers the car controls the radio." Guess who always steered the car when he was in the car? You got it. Plus, technology was working against me. In my day, you actually had to tune the radio—fiddle with the dial and land that red line on your station. Today, all kids have to do is hit a button and *bang,* they've got their station. Of course, there's always a fight in the car. Is it Barney, Lauryn Hill, or the traffic report? While Leila is much too young to reach the radio button, she can be heard from her car seat.

I look in my rearview mirror and see both

my girls. It wasn't that long ago that Courtney was in the car seat. So no matter how nutty the ride gets, as long as they are *in* the car, I feel lucky and blessed.

THE CRYING GAME

Leila was for a while a world-champion sleeper. From about three months till her first birthday, her sleeping habits made us the envy of other parents. I heard from friends that their three- and four-year-olds didn't sleep as much as Leila did.

That's why her new sleep patterns have thrown us for a bit of a loop. I feel as if she's sucker-punched Mom and Dad. "Hey, you two! Look at my thumb!" POW!!

After dropping off to sleep around seven-thirty or eight o'clock, lately Leila has been waking up at around two or three in the morning and crying. Not just crying but C-R-Y-I-N-G!! You've heard it—the one that starts with a wail, then goes silent as air rushes in to fuel the second half of the cry. You can almost count: one one thousand, two one thousand, three one thousand...and there it is, the downbeat of the cry. A long plaintive scream that undulates like the siren on a Parisian police car.

Here's where the difference between mothers and fathers comes in. Deborah's first reaction is to bolt upright in bed, make sure what she heard was, in fact, Leila and not some incredibly annoying car alarm that has pierced the night air, and race into the nursery. My first reaction is to hold Deborah down!

We are of two minds when it comes to Leila's waking up at night. Deborah wants to go to her and make sure that she's okay and that brigands haven't stolen into her room, trying to abscond with her, or that some closet monster hasn't materialized, trying to scare the bejeezus out of our infant. I, on the other hand, want to lie there and listen for a few minutes to see if she will put herself back to sleep.

If, after five minutes, Leila doesn't settle back down, Deborah breaks my hold and goes in to our baby. Her procedure is to soothe her, pick her up, rock her to sleep, and gently lay her back in the crib and tiptoe back to our bedroom.

That works, except for the laying her back

down part. Leila wakes up, eyes and mouth open. Guess which makes more noise? Deborah then picks her up and repeats the procedure, once, twice, three times more. Doesn't work. Checks the diaper, gives her a bottle. Still the air-raid siren is going full bore. Now, exasperated, exhausted, and frazzled after an hour of this, Deborah comes back to bed and we listen to Leila's siren song for about fifteen or twenty minutes.

Guess what? She cries herself to sleep. Five minutes after that, I'm asleep. Deborah, a light sleeper, is now wide awake. Why? Because she's completely rattled after Leila's performance, and she's ticked off at me for holding her back, being right about letting Leila cry, *and*, on top of all that, having the audacity to fall back to sleep.

Fathers are more pragmatic about this stuff. We roughhouse with our kids, boys or girls. We let them take more risks and we let them cry a little more. Especially when Daddy has to get up in about two or three hours.

Here's the irony of the whole thing. Before we were married, Deborah would always dismiss parents of crying or whiny children as "spineless wimps." "Why don't they discipline that baby? They probably pick it up as soon as it cries." I would comment to her, "Wait'll you have your own. You'll see." "Not me. I'm going to be the drill sergeant in this relationship. I know you're too soft," she would reply.

Hey, Sarge...drop and give me twenty. In

153

fairness to her, Deborah has toughened up some. She has let Leila cry for five or ten minutes at a time. But it's only because she is completely wiped out and just can't get out of bed.

I've conducted scientific studies, mainly at parties and social events, about this phenomenon. When asked who lets the baby cry, the fathers' hands shoot up like a rocket. The mothers all sit there sheepishly grinning. It's yet another difference between the sexes. On the other hand, mothers can be sick as a dog and still take care of the family *and* go to work, while fathers get a little cold and we're down for the count and can't even take care of ourselves, let alone the family. Of course, that's not crying...that's whining.

Works for me.

SIBLING SITTING

In this era of two-career families, child care has become one of the most important issues facing couples and their families today. Maternity and family leave address the beginning of a child's life with his or her parents. The ability to bond with that child as it comes into your home, whether it is a birth child or adopted, is very important.

But eventually you may have to leave that child with somebody else. That's where child care comes in. When I was a kid, it wasn't called "child care." It was called baby-sitting. And more often than not, it meant that my brothers and sisters and I were dropped off at a relative's house or a neighbor came over to watch us. Those were different times. We actually knew our neighbors and we lived near relatives, whether it was aunts, uncles, or grandparents.

I loved it when we went to Aunt Monica's house, because there was a whole passel of kids our own age. And Aunt Monica let us eat the junk our mom would *never* let us eat before dinner—ice cream, cake, cookies, and all manner of chips and pretzels. The bonus was that Aunt Monica and her family lived with Grandpa and Grandma Smith, my mother's folks. So we got to see our grandparents, eventually got a buck from Grandpa to buy comic books, and then settled in to eat junk upstairs at Aunt Monica's. It was heaven.

Aunt Maryanne and her family lived with Grandma Roker. This was the beauty of the nuclear family. Everyone either lived with everyone else or lived near everyone else. We were within a twenty-minute drive of just about 90 percent of our entire family.

Today our families are spread out and don't have that easy access to family members, although, depending on your family, that might not be such a bad thing.

My parents actually planned for built-in baby-sitting. My sibs and I are three years apart, so by the time I was twelve years old, I had a nine-year-old brother and sisters age six, three, and under one. My folks had the baby-sitting thing under control. I actually looked forward to baby-sitting because my parents liked to go out dancing on Friday nights. Friday afternoons, they went food shopping and the fridge and pantry were never fuller than on Friday night. It was like a smorgasbord in our own home. You can see there was a pattern developing early on in my life. Most kids demanded money for baby-sitting. Me? I had a list of snack foods and cold cuts I wanted.

The other great thing about baby-sitting on Friday night was Johnny Carson. Growing up, I equated maturity with being able to watch *The Tonight Show*. My folks would get us off to bed and from the confines of the bedroom I shared with my brother Andrew, I could hear them laughing. In fact, nobody outside of NBC called it *The Tonight Show*. It was the *Johnny Carson Show* or, as you got older, *Carson*. What could be better? A full fridge and The Mighty Carson Art Players on the tube!

With that as a backdrop, I can recall only two really bad incidents during my baby-sitting career. Both involved Andrew. The first occurred when I was about thirteen and my parents had gone out on a Saturday night. Ten-year-old brother Andrew and I had grand plans to stay up that night to watch the Alfred Hitchcock thriller *Psycho*.

It would be showing on Channel 7 at 11:30 that night, following the local news. Heck, if we could watch the local news, *Psycho* was a walk in the park. Neither one of us had seen it, but we knew it was scary. Once our younger sisters had been hosed down and put to bed, we were going to make popcorn for an appetizer, nachos for dinner, then have ice cream and pound cake for dessert. Cool! Well, on their way out the door, Mom turns to me and says, "Make sure your brother *does not* watch *Psycho*. Do you both understand? DO NOT LET ANDREW WATCH *PSYCHO*!!!" We both dutifully shook our heads up and down, said yes, and immediately forgot the admonition the moment the lock clicked in the door.

Our sisters cooperated by dropping off to sleep by 9:30, and we were ready to roll. All the snacks were at the ready, and at the appointed hour, all the lights went out, the TV went on, and we were ready for *Psycho*. Well, everything was okay until the infamous shower scene.

Neither one of us said a word during that whole scene. The movie faded to black and the TV station went to a commercial. I turned to my brother to talk about the movie and he was staring at the screen, eyes as big as saucers. Without a word, he got up, turned off the television, turned on every light in the house, then sat in the middle of the living room. As far as I could tell, he didn't blink for two hours. In fact, he didn't move until he heard the key in the front door. Then he started screaming. My parents walked in, took one look at their screaming child, then looked at me. "I didn't know he was there. He snuck downstairs behind me. I never heard him. Honest!!!" That little episode cost me two weeks of television viewing.

The next little trouble spot came about a year later. My folks were out for the day with my sisters in tow, so Andrew and I had the run of the house. This was the mid-1960s, when James Bond, *The Man from U.N.C.L.E.*, and *Secret Agent* were big. So we were home practicing our martial arts skills when my brother slipped and caught his head on the corner of the coffee table. Luckily, he only got a nasty little gash on the top of his head. It could've been a lot worse, but there was a fair amount of blood accompanying this wound.

Just as we were cleaning it out, we heard our parents' car pull up in front of the house. I dragged my brother into the kitchen and told him, "They are going to kill us." I looked at my brother's head and got an idea. "We were making lunch and things got out of hand," I said to him as I opened up the fridge and pulled out a bottle of ketchup. I squirted some on my shirt, on the kitchen table, and as the front door opened, on my brother's head to camouflage the gash in his head.

My mother pinned us with that mother look and my brother flipped quicker than Sammy "The Bull" Gravano. "The ketchup was Al's idea to hide the blood in my head." "He's delirious, Mom," I tried to salvage what seemed to me to be a perfectly good cover-up. "Andrew's so hungry, he's hallucinating. I was making sandwiches when the ketchup got stuck. I started hitting it on the bottom and the ketchup just went flying." My mother, looking at Andrew's scalp, said, "That ketchup must've really been flying to slice your brother's head like this." Busted!

And yet she still trusted me to watch my brothers and sisters after that. Let's face it, she knew that I loved them and would never let anything happen to them. That is, unless they started it first. And isn't that what a big brother is for?

Besides, where else was she gonna get someone to watch five kids for free?

OFF TO WORK

I was getting ready to go off on a trip, so I had come home after the *Today* show to pick up my bag, kiss Leila good-bye, and catch a cab to LaGuardia Airport. Turns out Deborah hadn't left for work yet, so as a bonus I was able to kiss her good-bye too.

I was headed out the door when Leila started fussing. I came back and hugged her and gave her another kiss and started for the door. Once again, a little tussle ensued, so Deborah scooped up Leila and headed with me to the elevator. After pushing the down button, we waited for the elevator to come, hugging and kissing the whole time.

DING! The door opened, I stepped in, and turned to wave to my little girl. She waved back to me and blew me a kiss. I thought I would melt as the elevator door slid shut. And that reminded me of my own childhood.

After a brief stay at Grandma Roker's, my folks moved into the projects in Rockaway, Queens, when I was about a year old. Only a block away from the beach, we lived on the fifth floor. My father was still a bus driver at that point, working the afternoon shift. Our routine never varied. When it was time for work, Dad put on his uniform, Mom handed him his lunch, and we walked out of the apartment to the elevator.

These were old-fashioned elevators with a window in the door. Dad would kiss me good-bye, get in the elevator, and Mom would hoist me up so I could watch the elevator car descend. Then, when it dropped out of sight, we would walk to the common terrace and wait for Dad to emerge from the building and walk into our line of sight. He would turn and wave, and we would wave back and keep waving until he disappeared around the corner.

I hadn't thought about that until I watched Leila wave good-bye to me. There is something special about that moment. Courtney would stand at the window of our family room, waving while I backed the car out of the garage. Then she'd run to the living room, open the front door, and wave bye-bye till my car turned the corner.

Most good-byes went pretty well. There was one that I will never forget. When Courtney was two and a half, the Sunday *Today* show moved to Washington, D.C., in an effort to save money. So each Saturday evening, a car would pick me up to take me to LaGuardia and the Delta Shuttle to Washington. One Saturday, Courtney was especially clingy. When it was time to go, she grabbed on to my legs with all her might and looked up at me imploringly and said, "Daddy, don't go!" I looked down at her and said, "Sweetheart, Daddy will be back tomorrow, okay?" With tears rimming those big brown eyes, she replied in a tiny little quivering voice, "But Daddy...I need you now." Uh, sweetheart, could you rip Daddy's heart out, chop it up into little pieces, spread it on toast, slip it under the broiler, then serve it to me?

So I never take good-byes for granted.

THE WAY IT IS

One of my favorite singer-songwriters is Bruce Hornsby. One of his early hits was a song called "The Way It Is." It's a song about life and racism and how people just accept that that's the way it is, that some things will never change. I think of the lyrics to that song as I watch Leila playing with some kids her own age. We've been going to a play-group at the 92nd Street Y here in Manhattan, and it's a highlight of our week. She has a little posse that she runs with and they are a delightful group of children who are growing up together.

I love looking at kids' faces as they discover each other. Leila usually has her hair up in a bun, fastened with a barrette that's color-coordinated by Evette. Thanks to her baby-sitter, she is normally the real fashion plate of the group. I remember the first day, and a couple of the babies crawled over to Leila and started patting her bun, while she started stroking their hair. After they explored each other's faces, they proceeded to start tearing the place apart.

Why can't we be more like them? We can acknowledge each other's differences, then move on. At this age, they don't care about skin color, eye shape, hair texture, or parents' religion. It's just about how well they play together and who has the toy that the other one wants and how to get it away.

Growing up for a time in a predominantly white project, I was taunted and teased. It was difficult, but my folks made me feel safe and secure. They made me feel that I was as good as anybody. In 1960, while I was in kinder-garten, there was a protest staged by blacks and Jews, upset by the fact that black kids were being kept out of the local public school,

P.S. 272. A boycott was organized and Jewish kids and minority kids were taught by an ad hoc group of teachers at the local synagogue. Eventually, the school board promised to make sure no one was steered away from the school.

People were banding together for the common good just at the beginning of the civil rights movement of the 1960s. I was five years old. I didn't know what it all meant. All I knew was that something was wrong, some people did something about it, and then it was better.

Growing up through the 1960s and 1970s, I really believed that our generation was going to make a difference, and in many ways it did. But certain things don't change, and it seems as if they never will. Racism is a problem that our country will not face. We pay lip service to it and dance around it, but it does not change.

During my freshman year of college, my first roommate was a nice guy who happened to be white, from Long Island. His name was Chris. I had arrived and unpacked my stuff before he did. I was sitting on my bed when he walked in. We exchanged greetings and names. An awkward silence ensued. After about five minutes, he looked at me and said, "So, you're black."

A nice guy, but he didn't get it. He wasn't willing just to accept me as a person. I would drone on and on about my family. One day he had this quizzical look on his face. "What? What's the matter?" I asked him. "It's just that

I never knew that blacks had such normal lives," he replied. "What? Lemme get this straight," I said, incredulously. "I'm the first black person you've really talked to, yet you're surprised that I have a 'normal' life? Look at you. Your folks are divorced, and you can't stand your brother or sister! I guess all white people come from broken homes."

"Awww, come on, Al. That's not what I meant. It's just that you're different," he countered. I could not believe what I was hearing. "So just how many black guys did you hang out with in high school?" Turns out, none. Why? "Well, they all had these angry looks on their faces." There's a shock. Who wouldn't look ticked off all the time, having to deal with nitwits like him?

But I assumed that by the time I had children, this would all be different. And I believed that, right up until the time Courtney, who was in third grade at the time, knocked me back into reality.

I had picked her up from school and we were driving back into the city when she asked me, "Daddy, what's a nigger?" It took every ounce of strength for me to keep the car from swerving. Holding my voice in check, I inquired, "Hmmmm, well, let me ask you something, sweetheart. Why do you ask that?" "Well," she replied, "Janie White [a name change here] said that I was a nigger. What's that?" My mind was now racing. Is this possible? Could one of her classmates actually have called her that? Did that child even know what it meant?

"Courtney, a nigger," I started carefully, "is a name that some really mean people use to describe black people. It's an ugly word used by ugly people. If anybody says that to you, you tell them it's a word used by mean, ugly people and that it's not nice." She looked like she was going to cry. "Daddy, does that mean Janie is mean and ugly?" This was 1993, mind you, not 1963. "No, sweetheart, it means Janie heard that word and repeated it, but probably doesn't know what it means."

That seemed to satisfy her, but I was seething. I knew exactly what had happened. This little girl heard this word bandied about in her home by a relative or a family friend and just assumed it was okay to use. It certainly was nice to know that someone of my generation was helping to perpetuate hateful language with their children so that it could continue to thrive into the next millennium.

That night, when I got home and Courtney was asleep, I pulled out her class list with the home phone numbers listed and called the Whites. Janie's mother answered. I identified myself and told her what happened and what was said. There was silence on the other end of the phone. I continued, telling her how hurtful this was to Courtney and to me, and that somebody in her home was exposing her daughter to hateful, poisonous language and that she should know about it. Again, silence. "Mrs. White, are you there?" Finally, she spoke. "Mr. Roker, I apologize for this and

I'm going to have Janie apologize to Courtney. I promise you that it will never happen again."

"Can I ask you who is saying these things in your home?" I queried.

"Let me just say, it's not me, and Janie's an only child."

We hung up, and it just amazed me that even if somebody feels like using that sort of language, they would do it in front of their children. It's like smoking around a child. Eventually it hurts them in ways you can never imagine.

I watch Leila play with her band of babies and I wonder at what point their differences will start affecting their perceptions about each other. When will their skin color, eye shape, hair texture, or parents' religion separate them? I'd like to believe never. But just when I start feeling that, a cab passes me by. Why? Because the cabbie is afraid to pick up an African-American male, no matter how well he's dressed, going downtown or uptown. That's just the way it is; some things will never change.

But then I remember more of the lyric: "...Ah, but don't you believe it!" I want to believe that things will change. As I see Leila cavorting with her hearty band of babies, there is hope that she and her friends will make a difference, that they will lead the charge of harmony and justice.

Most people see the horrific crimes of the three white Texans who dragged James Byrd Jr. to his death behind a pickup truck because he was black, or the beating death of gay college student Matthew Shepard, as hate crimes that should never be tolerated.

But as horrible as those crimes are, it's the little slights and cuts because of race, religion, or country of origin that inflict damage day in and day out. A child who hears a parent or loved one referring to some ethnic group or sexual orientation in a negative way will embrace those feelings as "the way it is." Only by refusing to tolerate hateful, negative speech or deeds, however small, can we change the foundation of the future: our kids.

"GAPKIDS ADDICT"

"Hi, my name is Al."

"Hi, Al!!!!"

"It's been thirty-seven days since I've been inside a GapKids store!" The applause washes

over me as I stand before my GapKids Anonymous meeting. My addiction, while always
there, has been in check for more than a
month now....

I suddenly awake from this nightmare and
sit bolt upright in bed, sweating profusely. Deborah asks me what's wrong. Nothing, I tell her,
just a bad dream.

I confess to you here and now: I am a Gap-
Kids addict. It is an obsession that started with
Courtney some eight years ago, when The
Gap added a kids' line to their stores. I don't
know about your town, but here in Manhattan there are more Gap stores than there
are Starbucks. If The Gap and Starbucks
ever decided to take over the world, we'd all
be caffeine-drinkin', khaki-wearin' zombies.

The Gap plays into the notion that we want
our kids to be small versions of us. Kind of like
our own personal versions of Dr. Evil's Mini-
Me. We see the little jeans, the little khakis,
the little dresses and skirts, and we go,
"Awwwwww." Who can resist? And lemme tell
you, while the boys' stuff is nice, the GapKids
stuff for girls just melts your heart. It sucks
you in, grabs you by the throat, and says,
"Your little girl would look so *cute* in this
and you're a fool if you don't buy it, even if
it is the same price as the adult version!!"

Who can argue with that?

So I began dressing Courtney in all this
GapKids stuff and of course folks would see
her and fawn all over her and coo and note that
her father had exquisite taste and how won-

168

derful it was that Daddy knew how to shop for his daughter. I was like that carnivorous plant in *The Little Shop of Horrors*. FEED ME!!! The seeds of my addiction were being insidiously planted and now taking root.

The closest thing we had to GapKids when I was growing up was Garanimals. It was simplicity itself. Animal tags on the various pieces of clothing were color-coordinated. Match the lion tag on the shirt with the lion tag on the pants and you were golden. Garanimals were made for kids and for those adults who were pattern-challenged. Garanimals would never let you mix and match stripes with polka dots or checks with plaids.

At first, it wasn't too bad because there weren't that many Gap stores around. They hadn't invaded the malls, the streets of our cities, the Internet. You could avoid them, if you wanted to. But I didn't want to. I needed to shop at GapKids. I saw a little girl wearing this to-die-for denim jacket. I thought, Courtney would look fab in this. Gotta get it. Of course, Courtney, at six, couldn't really care less where her clothes came from. That wouldn't come until much later.

At first, the kids' stuff was in the back. Then they started displaying the children's line in the front windows along with the adult clothing. The final denouement: creating stand-alone GapKids stores. I never stood a chance. Week after week, I would come home with bags of clothing: pants, sweaters, skirts, dresses, shoes, underwear, swimsuits, scrunchies. You name it, if it had GapKids on the label, I bought it.

All that changed. My family became concerned about me and staged an intervention. Fast-forward to last year. I was issued an edict. I am not allowed to shop for Courtney anymore. Here's how it went down. My methadone clinic to wean me from my GapKids addiction was catalog shopping from Lands' End: good, solid, well-made clothing at reasonable prices. Nothing trendy. The only problem was that at thirteen years old, Courtney refused to wear it. "Dad, what is this stuff? Are you serious?" She looked at Deborah for sympathy as I proudly took the clothes from the just-delivered box and opened the hermetically sealed plastic bags the outfits came in. "Hey, lookit these, Court! Pretty cool, huh?" showing her the denim jumper I had selected.

"Uh, sweetheart, those are very nice," Deborah interrupted. "But I need to talk to you in the bedroom for a minute," she said, leading me out of the family room and away from the visibly upset thirteen-year-old. It was then that Deborah explained the facts of clothing life. "Do not buy clothes for Courtney. She doesn't have your taste in clothing anymore. Doesn't matter if it's cute or hip or happening. If *you* buy it, it stinks."

I was crushed. What was I to do? I couldn't go to The Gap, I couldn't order from a catalog, and I couldn't order on-line for Courtney. That's when I heard Leila crying over the baby monitor. LEILA!!!

She's too young to argue. I can transfer my addiction... I mean, my desire to dress a daughter in stylish, overpriced clothing. Leila's too young to fight me on this. Heck, at a year and a half, she still confuses me with the Teletubbies. So, all is well in our home. Deborah can take Courtney shopping. I show up once a week at our apartment carrying a bag or two bulging with stuff from GapKids and everybody's happy. Especially Gap stockholders.

BALLPARK PLUMPING

"Did you and Pop-Pop come here when you were a little boy?" Courtney asked as we settled into our seats at her first baseball game. "We sure did, sweetie," I replied. And that question brought to mind my first excursion to the fabled Stadium—Yankee Stadium. For those of you who are from the planet Uranus, the Stadium is in the Bronx. We New Yorkers refer to Yankee Stadium as the Stadium. If you're going to see the Mets play, you're going to see them at Shea.

I remember, it was my dad, my brother Andrew, and my uncle Charlie. We left from Queens and took the subway. It seemed to take forever. I was about eight years old at the time.

We got to the game and I was in awe. I had seen Yankee Stadium on television, but it was nothing compared to actually being there. I remember it so well. It was a beautiful day. We were in the bleachers—the cheap seats. The sky was crystal clear. It was September, just a hint of coolness in the air. And I remember vividly my first words upon sitting in my seat in that hallowed baseball mecca: "Dad, can I have a hot dog?"

Two hot dogs, a box of Cracker Jack (candy-coated popcorn, peanuts, and a prize—that's what you get in Cracker Jack!), a soda, and a bag of peanuts. Have you ever been to the ballpark and you get those peanuts salted and roasted in the shell? Roasted so that the peanut's sweetness comes out. Uncle Charlie looked at me with disgust and said, "So, didja come here to watch baseball or to eat?" I thought, Is this a trick question? My uncle said to me, "Little Al, you are in the House that Babe Ruth Built." "Baby Ruth? The candy bar?" I asked him.

I can't tell you who the Yankees played that day, whether they won or lost. All I know is, I wanted one of those famous Yankee hot dogs—hot dogs that had a snap when you bit into them, with that brown-speckled mustard. I wanted the peanuts, the popcorn. Baseball was a means to an end. I got to spend time with my father and I got great food. Well, it was great food to an eight-year-old.

Nowadays, you go to a baseball game and

you can get sushi, natural food, hoagies, and French cuisine. What is this world coming to? There should be a law, limiting baseball stadium menus to peanuts, hot dogs, and Cracker Jack. Beer and soda go without saying.

Just then, Courtney roused me from my reverie. "Dad," she asked, "can I have some nachos?" Nachos? Sacrilege! So I gave her some more peanuts and told her to watch the game. After all, did we come here to eat or to watch a ball game?

SO WHAT'S THE DEAL WITH THESE TV RATINGS?

I don't quite get the hoopla. Different television groups want the networks to rate the shows they put on the air so that parents will know what shows to let their kids watch and what shows they should ban.

I've got a really nutty idea. How about making the parents watch the shows in question themselves and then they can decide whether or not they want their kids watching said shows?

Duh!

When I was a kid and started whacking my brother on the head in the hopes that his head would make the same sound as Curly's did when Moe bopped him on the labonza, my folks banned Stooge-watching in our house. Then my parents decided to take this experiment even further and banned us from watching television Monday through Thursday. We could watch from Friday after school until Ed Sullivan was over on Sunday night.

Well, our grades went up and our parents were busy congratulating themselves. Our friends all thought my brother and I were chumps, getting shut out of television during the week. And then our lives took a nasty turn. My parents started talking to some of the other parents on the block about this TV ban idea. Suddenly our friends were getting shut out of prime TV viewing, and they blamed us because our parents had told their parents. We became the two most hated kids on the block.

It was like the mob scene from *Frankenstein*: TV-deprived kids carrying pitchforks and torches... "There they are...the Roker kids. They're why we can't watch *Batman* on Wednesdays and Thursdays... GET 'EM!!!"

So I am sensitive to the fact that my daughter may think I'm an old fuddy-duddy when it comes to television and movies that I think might be questionable. Right now I'm in a pitched battle with Courtney about what shows and movies I think she should watch and what flicks and TV shows she thinks she can be able to watch. Before I let her watch a particular show on TV, I watch it to determine whether or not I think it's appropriate. As far as movies, well, the movie ratings and I disagree a bit. What they think is appropriate under the PG-13 banner I often find to be a little closer to PG-16 or -18.

I don't know what words thirteen-year-olds are supposed to be using, but in some of these movies that get rated PG-13, those youngsters could teach a marine or a longshoreman a thing or two.

If I can't see the movie first, I ask someone I trust who may have seen the movie if it's appropriate for a thirteen- or fourteen-year-old. I embarrassed Courtney recently when I asked Jeffrey Lyons, WNBC's movie critic, on the air if he would let his twelve-year-old daughter see *Sleepy Hollow*. Jeffrey replied, "No, I wouldn't and you shouldn't let Courtney see it either!" She was mortified. I was thrilled. I got validation and it was on record in front of the whole Tri-state area that Courtney should not go to see this R-rated movie.

Now, I know that as parents you can't watch every show, and some viewing guidelines are helpful. But let's also exercise our right and responsibility as parents to know what our kids are watching, what video games they're playing, and what the parents of friends or relatives let their kids watch.

And what about the shows we as parents watch with our kids around? Deborah pointed out to me that an animated show like *Futurama*, which uses the words *ass* and *bastard* quite liberally, may not be a show I want Courtney watching with me (although I think it's a hoot).

175

Of course there is always the unthinkable. We could give permission to look at that special something with an R rating: a book. You know, R...as in Read. Oh, the horror!!

DADDY-IN-A-BOX

I have spent most of my adult life doing television weather. I started at the end of my sophomore year at Oswego State University in 1974 when I got a job doing weekend TV weather for WHEN-TV. I was just as shocked as my college professor, who had recommended me for the job, when I got it. I was making $10 a newscast back then, big money for a college sophomore.

I never intended to be on TV. True story: My department chairman, the guy who recommended me for the job, Dr. Louis B.

O'Donnell, was like a god to all of us Radio/TV majors. One day during TV Production, a class I shared with Jerry Seinfeld, "Doc," as we called him, looked at my mug on a monitor and proclaimed, "Roker! You have the perfect face for radio!"

Yes, I glossed over the fact that Jerry Seinfeld and I went to the same college. Although he did ultimately graduate from Queens College in New York City, his freshman and sophomore years were spent at Oswego State. Jerry was a studious guy who worked on writing his stand-up material constantly. I have always said he might've really made something of himself had he stuck it out for the full four years at Oswego.

Unlike Jerry, being on TV was not my goal. I wanted to be a writer or director. To make extra cash at WHEN, I did graphics for news and commercials. I didn't think for a minute that I could really make a living as a weatherman. But it seemed to stick, and here I am some twenty-six years later doing the weather.

As far as Courtney and Leila are concerned, I have been on television all their lives. Their dad is somebody other people know. I'm not sure how good a thing that is, but it's something they have to deal with.

When Courtney was much younger, I did the weather on the 5, 6, and 11 P.M. news on WNBC, which freed up my mornings. I was able to get up with Courtney. I got her bathed, dressed, and ready for preschool. I treasured those mornings. We had breakfast and watched some *Sesame Street.* We consulted each other about lunch and other important issues of the day. Having free mornings allowed me to volunteer at Courtney's preschool.

While her classmates' parents would ask about the upcoming weekend weather, the only thing her fellow preschoolers would ask of me was to open a recalcitrant yogurt top or thermos. It's funny, but most of Courtney's friends never thought much about my being on television because they really knew me only as Courtney's daddy.

As Courtney got older, she and her pals realized that I was on TV. I always stressed that being on television was no big deal. Showing up on someone's TV didn't make you better or smarter or better lookin' than anyone else. It's a job, like anybody else's mother or father has. It's just that my job is on TV. Case closed.

But as the years have progressed, it's been harder and harder for Courtney. When her mother and I separated and eventually divorced, it was fodder for the local newspapers. Divorce is hard enough for a child. Add the microscope that a "celebrity" couple gets put under, and it becomes that much harder. All of her friends knew about it, because their parents read about it in the papers.

When Courtney was about six, we were at a local amusement park one summer day. For some reason, we were inundated by fans and well-wishers. She came close to being knocked down. The park's head security officer came over and asked me if I wanted some protection. Hey, I'm no Michael Jackson here. First of all, I'm still black. I don't travel with a security team. But it was a sobering moment. Courtney saw her father in a different light. She asked me, "Daddy, why were all those people so rude?" I thought for a second and said, "Sweetheart, people sometimes want to be able to talk to people who are on television. They think people like me are someone they'd like to know because they see us on TV." Courtney looked quizzically at me and then replied, "But don't they know you're just Daddy?"

I think she's done a pretty good job processing the idea that her father is on television. However, that wasn't always the case. Once, when she was about eighteen months old, we were all home on New Year's morning, which happened to fall on a Sunday. Normally I would be at NBC doing the Sunday *Today* show, but Sunday's show had been taped so we could all recover from New Year's Eve.

Courtney, her mom, and I were in the family room watching the show, when I got up to go get something out of the kitchen. By this time, Courtney could recognize Daddy on television. When I would come up on screen, she would clap her hands and shout "DA-DA! DA-DA!" Kind of like Daddy-in-the-box. Well, sure enough, after I left the room, up popped Daddy on television. I heard her squealing and clapping her hands. Since I'm normally on TV live, I had never witnessed this, so I rushed back into the family room to see it.

Courtney peered up at me and suddenly a look of panic crossed her face. There, for the first time she saw Daddy-in-the-box and Daddy-in-person at the same time. Her little head swiveled from me to the television, back to me, and then back to the TV. And then she broke into tears. She had never seen both daddys together.

I have to admit I was thrilled again when several people, including Leila's baby-sitter, Evette, told me that when I pop up on TV, Leila starts squealing and crawls over to the television and says, "DA-DA! DA-DA!" Of course, it annoys her mother no end. At ten months old, Leila still hadn't said "Ma-ma" yet. Hey, Deborah got to breast-feed, I get name recognition. I think it's an even exchange. My wife represented boob food, and Leila sees me on the boob tube.

TOON QUESTIONS

Out of the mouths of babes!

Earlier this year, on a rainy Saturday evening, Courtney wanted to watch a video with me. Just thrilled that my teenager decided to actually do something with me, I jumped at the chance. We hemmed and hawed and finally decided to go with the classics...*Space Jam*. As I already mentioned, I am a huge toon fan. I love animation.

While it isn't *Who Framed Roger Rabbit* or *The Lion King, Space Jam* is fun, furious, and faboo. Michael Jordan is a charming and charismatic performer, just as you might imagine him to be. The film is technically flawless—both traditional and computer animation are seamlessly melded with live action.

However, while watching it, Courtney voiced a question that had been dancing around the back of my head for a long time.

"Dad," she asked, "why does Bugs Bunny wear gloves?" I sat there for a moment and gave her the best, most honest answer I could. "I don't know, sweetheart." And it was a question that has bothered me to this day.

Accepting the fact that a rabbit can talk, and a pig can stutter, why do they wear gloves? Why does Bugs Bunny wear gloves? I asked that very question during an interview with the legendary animator and director Chuck Jones. He told me why toons usually have only three fingers and a thumb: easier to animate, saves time. But he couldn't tell me why a lot of the classic toons like Mickey and Bugs and Woody Woodpecker wear gloves.

And who decides which character wears pants? Mickey always wears pants, yet Donald just wears that sailor shirt. Porky has a jacket and a bow tie, but no shirt or pants, and Daffy just has his feathers.

And I think it's accepted that Goofy is a dog. But so is Pluto. How did Goofy make the evolutionary leap to stand up on his hind legs, put on pants, a shirt, and a vest, and talk (albeit like a hayseed, but still talk)? Pluto, on the other hand, was content to stay in the backyard and hang out in the doghouse getting his butt kicked by Chip 'n Dale.

And while we're at it, explain this: If Wile E. Coyote could order all this stuff from Acme, why didn't he just order food?

Look, I know, you're thinking, Roker...get a life! These are cartoons. They are not real. I know that, but you gotta realize, as a teenager, these were the kinds of conversations I had with my friends. Who was faster: Superman or the Flash? Who would win head-to-head: The Mighty Thor or the Incredible Hulk? These questions were never resolved. Some folks are looking for the meaning of life. Me, I'm looking for the meaning of gloves.

THE MOST IMPORTANT OF ROOMS

The goal of every generation is for their children to be better off and to have more stuff than they had. To me, there is no greater example of this phenomenon than having more than one bathroom. When I was growing up, my father would tell us tales of having to walk three miles to the nearest outhouse...in a raging blizzard...in July. We should appreciate having toilet tissue. To hear him tell it, he didn't realize newspapers were actually meant to be read until he went to high school.

He would launch into these examples of having to do without when we would complain that we only had one bathroom, while our friends had bathrooms on the first floor, second floor, in the basement, and even, I suspect, in the doghouse in their backyard.

183

In reality, having one bathroom wasn't the worst thing in the world. Even with just that one water closet, it was viewed as an island of peace in a world gone mad...our house. Six kids and two adults can get a little testy when squeezed into a three-bedroom house. In our home, however, the bathroom was looked upon as sacred ground.

It was located on the second floor of our home, and Dad called it "the reading room," a place he could take the newspaper or the latest issue of *Ebony* and relax and take care of business.

Once in a while my mother would call upstairs, "Al, how long are you going to be in there?" He would call back down through the door, "Last I checked, nobody died and made you timekeeper!!"

The only time a one-bathroom house was a pain in the keester was when we would come home from a trip to the beach. Did I mention I hate the beach? I like the ocean, I like water, I don't mind going across the sand to get to the water. I hate being *on* the beach. The sand gets everywhere. When we were kids and we went to the beach, no matter how much my mother wrapped our sandwiches in plastic wrap or foil, sand got inside. I used to think that's why they were actually called *sand*wiches. Whether it was ham and cheese or peanut butter and jelly, they had a little grit, thanks to the sand. Peaches, apples, ice cream, and potato chips all had that little something extra.

And sand got in your bathing suit. No matter how hard I tried to avoid it, I'd get a suit full of sand. Because Mom was deathly afraid that other people's germs would contaminate her children, we weren't allowed to use the public showers. And if you had to use the lavatory at the beach, we were taught how to drape toilet tissue on the toilet seat to avoid any unpleasant germs lurking there as well. To this day, if a public bathroom doesn't have those paper toilet seat covers, I make my own out of toilet tissue. In any event, the car ride home was a festival of salty, squirming, sandy children.

Once home, it was time to hose off the kids. Being the oldest, I had to wait until my five brothers and sisters got cleaned off. Normally, my mother's policy was that each person had to clean the tub after his or her bath or shower. That rule was usually suspended on bath hose-down days, so by the time I got to the tub, the sand on the bottom was about six inches deep. You could make sand castles with what was in the bottom of that tub.

With that in mind, I always promised myself that when I was on my own, I would have a house with more than one bathroom. My children wouldn't have to wait for their old man to finish the latest article in *Entertainment Weekly* before they could go.

Of course, the problem with that is you miss the sense of community and motivation the single-bathroom household provides. Forget about an alarm clock. The need to get to the bathroom first will get you out of bed faster than any alarm. And you can always catch up with your brothers and sisters while you're waiting your turn in the loo.

Even with three bathrooms in our apartment, Courtney doesn't think she has enough privacy, and I know that's because of the teen thing. She would be happier if her bathroom were a little farther away from ours, say, in Montana. I might knock on her bathroom door if I hear her in there washing up, and I hear the door lock thrown and she peeks through a tiny crack with a very tentative "Yes?" I know she's not doing anything illicit in there, I just may have had a question, but I have invaded her privacy.

I'm thinking of closing up two of our bathrooms to get back to the basics. The heck with wanting your kids to have it better than you did. I think my daughters should also have the pleasure of knowing that there just may be somebody lurking on the other side of that door, waiting with a magazine in hand.

THE GREAT VEHICLE DEBATE

I will admit it right now, as you read this: I want a minivan. I make no secret that I look at these variations on the great Econoline vans and step vans of my parents' day, and I covet them.

I know that this is not something that most adults would admit to, but I like the idea of being able to transport all at once three or four children, two adults, and the contents of a no-holds-barred shopping trip to BJ's Warehouse or Costco.

There's only one thing standing in the way of achieving my goal: Deborah. She refuses to get inside a minivan. It's not that she's a snob, she just never pictured herself in one. She is not a "soccer mom." She's a mom, and Leila or Courtney may play soccer, but she isn't a soccer mom. If she played soccer, then she'd be a soccer mom.

It took me a couple of years to convince her that sport utility vehicles were a necessity. When we first started dating, I had a Ford Explorer. I had it when I was still living in the suburbs and I got it as part of my divorce settlement. Deborah looked at it with disdain, until I picked her up after one of her shopping excursions. My wife looks at clothes shopping as a full-contact sport. It's not enough that she succeed; you—as another woman competing for the same piece of clothing—must fail miserably.

It was following one of these fashion campaigns that I met her on Madison Avenue with my truck. Until then, she complained about the ride. "This thing rides like a truck," she proclaimed. "That's because...it *is* a truck, sweetheart." She whined and moaned about the rough ride, the bumps and rolls, until she saw how much it could hold after a full day of shopping. In fact, she was so impressed, she jumped out and hit a couple more stores because there were still a few nooks and crannies left in the truck.

So I've been able to move her from a passenger car to an SUV without much difficulty. But I tipped my hand when she noticed large white envelopes coming to the apartment with different vehicle manufacturers' names on them like Ford, Chrysler, and Honda. Her curiosity piqued, she inquired as to what kind of cars I thought might replace our current truck, a Land Rover Discovery. "Ohhh, I don't know. I haven't really thought about it." "Oh, really," she said. "Then what are...THESE??" she exclaimed, pulling out the brochures extolling the virtues of all kinds of minivans from underneath a couch cushion. Busted!

"We are not getting a minivan. Period," she declared. "But," I countered, "we need the room. Courtney wants to invite friends to the apartment, Leila has all this stuff we have to carry, and we need room for groceries." Deborah just shook her head and walked away, leaving me to fantasize about the Chrysler Town and Country or the Honda Odyssey.

I remember my first SUV with fondness. It was my first truck and I loved the manliness of it. It was a 1990, the first year the Explorer came out.

When I pulled into my driveway, I was instantly the envy of all the guys in the neighborhood. Put a new truck in a neighborhood on a Saturday morning and it will draw men to that driveway like moths to a flame. My next-door neighbor was the first to be drawn into the Explorer's gravitational pull. "Hey, new truck, Al?" "Yep," I replied proudly. I did all the obligatory moves. I lifted the hood, started the engine, put my baby through the paces, and she performed like a champ.

Six years later, when I decided to give the truck to my sister because her family was moving to Cleveland, I had to clean my baby out, and I got very sentimental. Not because

I was losing my vehicle to a good cause, but because as I cleaned it out, it was like excavating Courtney's childhood. She was three years old when I first put her in it. Throughout the backseat and the cargo area, I found evidence of my daughter's growth. In the top layer was a discarded *Goosebumps* book. Digging a little deeper, I found disassembled Happy Meal toys and petrified French fries. As I moved down closer to the floor, there were Weebles (Weebles wobble, but they don't fall down), Little People, and pacifiers. I had a box for all the junk I was going to toss out, but I found that I couldn't part with any of it. It was my own archaeological dig of Courtney's childhood.

The same thing happened when I finally turned the Land Rover in. Leila's not-so-distant past was strewn across the cubbies and underside of the seats. Little rattles, tiny stuffed bears, and board books were everywhere. It all joined the box of Courtney's car stuff in the basement.

Maybe that's why I want the minivan. It's not so much about what it can carry, it's more about its capacity to keep things.

HOW QUICKLY WE FORGET

If there's one thing having children twelve years apart teaches you, it's that you forget a lot in twelve years. It's been twelve years since I had to take care of a baby. Twelve years since I looked into a tiny face and wondered what she will become. Twelve years since I held someone in the crook of my arm and supported her head with my hand.

It's been twelve years since I walked the floor with a screaming infant who would not go to sleep even though Daddy *really* needed to hit the sack and get up because he was on the air in three hours. Twelve years since I could see the future in two small dark orbs. Twelve years since I couldn't stop looking at the miracle of what a baby is all about.

It's been twelve years since I stood by the side of a crib and watched a little girl sleep. Twelve years since I felt helpless when this person who depends on you for everything looks up at you when she's sick, imploring you to make her feel better—and you can't.

It's been twelve years since I felt like a pack mule, lugging diaper bags and strollers and car seats around. Twelve years. Come to think of it, it seems like yesterday. I was thrilled to do it with Courtney and I'm just as thrilled twelve years later with Leila.

In some ways, it's like riding a bicycle. Holding Leila, it came back to me as if it were just yesterday that I had Courtney in my arms this way. It drives Deborah crazy the way I hold Leila. It's a little like holding a football—a football that moves, squirms, and drools. I still haven't met a baby who doesn't laugh like crazy when you lift their shirt and blow on that cute little belly...BRRRRRRPPPPPPP! Hey, I love it. I can't get Deborah to do it to me, but I'm still holding out hope. The smell of a freshly bathed baby, slathered with baby oil, is a scent no one can ever forget. Somebody ought to bottle it. Even those little feet smell good. However, I have to add: you remember reading about breast-fed babies having "sweet"-smelling poops? Right. Okay, it doesn't smell like a toxic waste dump, but there ain't nothin' sweet about that diaper.

Because it's been twelve years since I last had a baby in the house (Courtney is now a teenager), the problems I now have to deal with are a little different than those back then. I'd forgotten some of the rules of babyhood.

For example, if I've fed Leila, I shouldn't shake her, even if she's been burped. Of course, for fun, I could shake her, then hand her off to Deborah and watch her get tagged by baby spit-up. It's kind of like shaking up a can of Coke and then giving it to someone else to open. There also seems to be a direct relationship between how much spit-up you will get tagged with and how nice the clothing you're wearing is! Courtney was a champ at waiting till I was dressed for work, about to head out the door, and then BOOM! Baby Vesuvius would erupt and deposit a lovely pattern on my shoulder as I went to kiss her good-bye.

On a related topic, if you value your life, never walk into the room your wife is breast-feeding in and greet her with "Hello, Elsie!" This is especially important if your reflexes are a little rusty, because you will get caught upside the head with whatever is nearby and throwable.

I also forgot how much snot you can get inside such a tiny head. When a baby gets a cold, it's like a little mucus machine. It's the Eveready Bunny of mucus. It just keeps going and going and going. One of the things I hated to do with Courtney and I hate it just as much with Leila is suctioning her out. If you've ever had to do it, you know what I mean. There's a rubber bulb with a little nozzle on the end. You squeeze it, place it in your child's nostril, and then let go. The resultant suction will pull the offending mucus out of their nasal passages. The problem, of course, is that they don't want you to do it, so it's like wrestling a little octopus. Suddenly they are all arms and legs trying to thwart you from performing this hideous task. Deborah is over my shoulder saying, "Oh, you're hurting her. Let's stop." I'm thinking, Do you want to do what my dad did to us? My mother tells the story that because they were short of funds, they couldn't afford one of these devices, so my dad would actually put his mouth over my nose and suck it out himself. EEEWWWWWW!!! Man, do I owe my father big-time.

But I *do* know how good it feels to have your child look at you and smile—a grin that lights up her face and then yours. And it doesn't matter whether the girl is one or thirteen. It means the world to you. No matter what you forget or remember, all you know is, in that moment, it's all worth it.

IT'S HIP TO BE SQUARE

As I watched the MTV Video Awards, something became crystal clear to me. I had no idea—not a clue—of who 90 percent of these bands were. I had not heard their music, I did not know their names, and once I did hear their music, I was clueless as to their popularity. Then it hit me! I'm thinking things my dad used to say. "Buncha freaks!" "Who could dance to this stuff anyway? It's not like when we were coming up. Nat King Cole, Lloyd Price, Frank Sinatra, Ella Fitzgerald...now *that* was music!"

I am now listening to Lite-FM..."the best mix of the '70s, '80s, and today's favorites." I am one step away from digging elevator tunes. How did this happen? Why did it happen? I want my music played softer, while I ask people to speak up. Am I officially "middle aged"? I'm a living version of the Huey Lewis tune "Hip to Be Square."

Oh, for the days when I put on my bell-bottoms, love beads, and platform shoes and danced the night away to those hip, happenin' Delfonics. Now that was music.... Why, I remember when I was a boy...

This is about the time my kids, your kids, start fading out, thinking, When I'm a parent, I'm gonna be cool, and not bore *my* kids with this crap. Little do they know, that's what we thought too.

But I try to be a good dad and not let my bias get in the way of Courtney's having a good time.

Case in point: Recently, I took Courtney and two of her pals to a local radio station concert out at a sports arena in New Jersey. A very popular morning show, the Z Morning Zoo, and their hosts were celebrating their fourth anniversary.

I've been a frequent guest on the program and I like these guys. And, fortunately, they like me. At the height of the Ricky Martin mania they did a spoof of the song "Livin' La Vida Loca" called, "Talkin' About Al Roker." It was very cute and, more important, Courtney and her friends thought it was cool, so suddenly I was a big shot in my twelve-year-old's eyes. So they invited me to come to the concert as their guest and bring Courtney and a couple of her pals. I said yes.

What was I thinking?

First of all, I had three twelve-year-olds to deal with. One was my daughter, so what's the problem? Well, in theory that's correct. But have you ever had to deal with three twelve-year-old girls? It's no walk in the park. They speak a mile a minute, in a language that is closest perhaps to Farsi.

We get to the concert and we are two rows from the front. They are thrilled. I am dismayed as I look at tower speakers the size of a Manhattan high-rise. Luckily, a guard took pity on me and gave me a pair of earplugs.

The first act was...I can't even remember. I know Britney Spears was on the bill. Courtney and her friends like her music, but not the fact that she has allegedly had breast augmentation. Sugar Ray, 98 Degrees, and Joey McIntyre were faves because they are so darn cute. UB40, an English reggae band, was also on the bill. The girls found them boring, but since they've been around awhile, I actually dug the act. I think the radio station slipped them in for all the parents who were there with their kids.

The average audience member was female and between twelve and sixteen. It was a great place to be if you were a twelve- to sixteen-year-old boy. For this reason I was glad I was around, since the boys were checking out the girls, including my daughter.

All I remember was the sound. The bass from those speakers liquefied one or two of my internal organs. I have no recollection of the music, just the sound. I looked over at my little girl and saw how happy she and her pals were, and I just pushed the earplugs in deeper and sat back and enjoyed.

The next day I was whining to my mother about the concert and she reminded me that she had to do the same thing with me when I was Courtney's age.

The year was 1964. Soupy Sales was one of the legendary kids' TV hosts, first on ABC television out of Detroit and WXYZ-TV, later on Metromedia WNEW-TV Channel 5, here in New York City. A journalism major at the University of West Virginia, Soupy found his way into radio, then television.

A stand-up comic in the time-honored tradition of burlesque, Soupy eventually made it to the Big Apple as the host of the *Soupy Sales Show* back in the early 1960s. His TV show was a success with adults as well as kids, and he also recorded two Top-10 hits with "The Mouse" and "Paufalafaka." He sold out concerts at such legendary venues as the Paramount and Radio City Music Hall.

In 1964, he was so big, he was the headliner at the Singer Bowl on the grounds of the 1964 World's Fair. My mom took a buddy of mine, my brother, and me on the subway to go see my hero, Soupy Sales. I was ten at the time, and worshiped this guy. In fact, earlier that summer, I took second place in the Pepsi-Cola All City Parks Department Talent Show with my ventriloquist's dummy, Steven Stickyfingers. We did a rendition of "The Mouse," only to be beaten by four girls who lip-synched "I Wanna Hold Your Hand."

The irony is, that same night, over at Shea Stadium, who was playing against Soupy but those four moptops from Liverpool, THE BEATLES!!!

We were jammed into the Number 7 subway. It was packed with teens, young adults, and adults, most of whom were going to see the Beatles. My mom looks around at the crowd and says to us, "I had no idea this Soupy Sales was *so* popular!"

My mother had no clue as to why I liked Soupy Sales. She didn't think he was funny, didn't think he could sing, and didn't think he had any business corrupting her boys with mindless drivel like his television show. Yet there she was with her two boys and a neighbor's kid, sitting in the nosebleed section of the Singer Bowl, watching a grown man tell fifty-year-old jokes and get hit in the face with a pie. High-concept comedy to ten-year-olds.

And after my mother reminded me of the story, I realized that my taking Courtney to that concert was a rite of passage for both of us. I know she had a good time, and deep down, I did too, looking at her face, full of early teen rapture at seeing her singing idols up close, imagining that when Joey McIntyre looked in her direction, he was really looking at her.

Granted, I didn't regain full hearing for two days, but it was worth it. And just think, in a year or two, I'll get to do this with Leila. Only with her it'll be Barney. Hmmmm. On second thought, those Backstreet Boys are looking better and better. Or was it 98 Degrees, or 'N Sync?

I gotta start watching MTV more.

WHERE'S ROD SERLING WHEN YOU NEED HIM?

We've all seen the classic TV show *Kids Say the Darndest Things*. The first version was hosted by Art Linkletter. The latest incarnation has Bill Cosby at the helm. We laugh, knowing that our sweet little child has the potential to say something embarrassing.

Whose kid hasn't blurted out something you and your spouse talked about in the privacy of your own kitchen, only to have it drop like a smart bomb in the middle of a family gathering? A perfectly lovely afternoon with the in-laws, ruined when little Jane or Johnny talks about how Daddy thinks "Uncle Bob's rug looks like a small woodland creature stuck on his head." Or how about: "Mommy says you drink like a fish, Aunt Gertrude, but I see you drink out of a glass like everyone else."

It's the proverbial poop-in-the-punchbowl moment. There you are, hoping against hope that at that very second the earth would do you the very large favor of opening up and swallowing either you or the offended party, leaving nary a trace.

I've had a few of those, courtesy of Courtney. She's thirteen now, but in her toddler days, she could render a room speechless with a few of her baby bons mots. Unfortunately, at these moments it feels like a different classic TV show.

Picture if you will a universe where time and space stand still. A place where seconds seem like hours. A place called the Baby Zone. Maybe you've seen this show. Here are a few episodes that you may have caught.

Episode One

Submitted for your approval:
A father is driving with his two-year-old daughter safely ensconced in a child safety seat in the back of their vehicle. Although he lives in suburban New York, he grew up driving on the streets of Manhattan. He took Driver's Ed. in lower Manhattan. Weakness is not a virtue. Drive or be driven off the road. Therefore Courtney's daddy uses quite liberally the one offensive tool given to the driver...the horn. And each time Daddy's cut off, he lays on the horn and mutters an expletive that is associated with fecal matter. BEEP..."S★★T!" BEEP..."S★★T!" BEEP..."S★★T!" It was a regular routine until one day Daddy was driving as usual and somebody cut him off. Well, Daddy leaned on the horn and from the backseat came this tiny voice that said, "S★★T!" Needless to say, Daddy was a bit taken aback. He hadn't realized that he had a twenty-three-pound Sony tape recorder in the back.

A few days later, Mommy brought Courtney into New York City to visit Dad and have lunch with some friends at an outdoor café at

Rockefeller Center. Lunch was ordered and everyone was chatting, when up on the street, a traffic jam was obviously gumming things up. Just as Daddy was about to comment on the noise, the blaring horn of a truck pierced the air. Courtney looked up and said, "S★★T!"

The Mommy looked at the Daddy with eyes that said, Great. Thanks for expanding her vocabulary. Daddy then realized he'd better watch what he says around small ears. The other couple was embarrassed and Daddy looked around for a convenient sinkhole near the statue of Prometheus. Alas, none was evident, so he sheepishly excused himself to look for the nearest bathroom.

Episode Two

Submitted for your approval:
An average dad, standing in the bathroom, minding his own business, doing his own business, when his three-year-old daughter busts in the door. "Daddy...can I watch...oh, what's that?" she asks, pointing just below Daddy's midsection.

I don't know about you, but while my mother was quite explicit about calling organs what they were, my dad used nicknames, like "the woo-woo" or "the pee-pee." I'm comfortable with that. And I think most men are like me. We don't want to use the real word. We like nicknames. Women want to use the real names. Where's the fun in that? Nothing creative there.

Courtney's mother carried on that same tradition, while I fell squarely on the side of keeping reality at bay for as long as possible. Again, my daughter asked, "What is that, Daddy?" Trapped. Literally, nowhere to run. "Well, sweetie...that's Daddy's...Daddy's..." Just then Courtney's mom called out, "There's nothing to be ashamed of. Just tell her what it is." Looking at my daughter, as I zipped up and flushed the toilet, I said, "Sweetie, that's Daddy's...uh...pee-pee!" "Tell her what it's really called, Al!" came a reprimand from Alice. Busted. "It's Daddy's...penis." "I couldn't hear you, Daddy." This is a kid who could hear the Animaniacs on a television two blocks away, now suddenly she's hard of hearing! "It's Daddy's penis." "Oh, okay." And with that, she turned and left the bathroom. Whew. That wasn't so bad. Hmmmm. Maybe this calling things what they are isn't so bad after all.

Fast-forward to later that same day. Courtney and I are shopping at the local A&P. We're in the checkout line. There's an older lady behind us, waving to Courtney, who is sitting in the shopping cart. Courtney, being the social child she is, is waving back and smiling. Emboldened, the woman said to Courtney, "You are such a beautiful girl. And you have a daddy who's a big star on TV." And Courtney said, "Yes, I know, and he has a very BIIIG penis!" Did I hear the earth rumbling? Anybody see a convenient sinkhole near Aisle 6? I turned around to see a look of horror on this unsuspecting woman's face. Trying to repair the damage, I just smiled and said, "She's like one of those side-view mirrors. 'Objects are larger than they appear.' "

Episode Three

A year or so later, we were shopping for furniture in a large showroom. Courtney was just running wild in this store. As is always the case, possession of a child depends on the severity of his or her behavior. And so it was that Courtney's mother told me, "Your child is acting the fool. Go get your daughter!" Earlier in the day when she was napping, Courtney was our daughter. Now that she is terrorizing an entire shopping center, she's my sole possession.

So, I dutifully go after her. She's jumping over couches, bouncing off beds, and tumbling under tables like some stuntman in a Jackie Chan movie. Just as I catch up to her and am about to grab her, there's a lull in the Muzak playing throughout the store. It seems all conversation stopped just in time for Courtney to say, in a very loud voice and with a big grin on her face, "Oh, Daddy, please don't hit me in the face again!"

Every head in the place turned to see the brute who could lay a finger on such an angel. I am frozen in place, listening for the sound of the earth opening up in the dinette section. When the floor remained intact, cutting off the chance for any graceful escape, I just laughed and said, "She's such a kidder. Ha Ha...HA!" It's obvious she and her buddies were swapping stories at the Montessori day care center that would stop parents in their tracks. I even think she had the Child Abuse Hotline on speed dial as a threat. This kid's barely been swatted on her Huggies-padded rump, let alone hit. But in her little-kid world, this was a howl. Never mind that every time all those people at the store watched Daddy on the news, they would shake their heads and think unpleasant thoughts.

So, if you're raising a small child and you have to take them out in public where an embarrassing word or phrase could prove devastating, my advice to you is to try to schedule such outings around naptime. Barring that, check with your local geologic survey to see if there are any rumblings in the earth's crust in your area that might provide a handy getaway.

GOLDEN TIME

I love my daughters. I cherish the time I get to spend with each of them. I have Courtney for a limited time each month, and that time is very special to me.

Because of my job, I'm not home during the week to see Leila wake up. I'm treated to those moments only on the weekend, and I enjoy every minute of it. I'm reminded of similar times I shared with Courtney almost thirteen years earlier. From the illuminating smile that greets me when I enter the room, to that all-powerful scent that greets me when I unsnap her onesie and pull the adhesive tabs off her Pamper.

But there is a time that every parent comes to appreciate. A special time that descends upon them after a long day when their precious bundle has been particularly trying or difficult. A time that you, as a parent, embrace and love. I call it "Golden Time."

What is Golden Time? It's the first five minutes after all the kids are asleep and you slump down in your favorite chair or couch and let out a long, deep breath. You savor the silence that has descended upon your abode. You drink in the quiet most of which you gladly traded the second that tiny person entered your life.

Obviously, the more children in your house, the harder it is to achieve Golden Time. My parents had six of us running around with a span of seventeen years between my baby brother and me. For them, Golden Time might not occur until ten or eleven at night. In fact, my father would just fall asleep waiting for Golden Time. Most nights he gave up on the whole concept and just went to bed.

My parents had to wait forty-four years for the ultimate Golden Time. That's when my youngest brother, Chris, got married and moved out of the house. Now their whole day is nothing but Golden Time. Well, for my mom, Golden Time occurs when Dad goes out fishing. And for Dad, it's when Mom goes out bowling. But the point is, it took them a looooooooong time.

In the beginning, it is very hard to reach Golden Time with a newborn. The problem is, you know that the child is going to wake up again pretty soon. The question is...when? An hour? Two hours? Fifteen minutes? Who knows? So you can't settle in, take that deep breath, let it out, and just relax. You are still in a state of full readiness. At any moment, the air-raid siren sleeping in the next room could go off and you have to hit the ground running. Breast, bottle, diaper, whatever he or she needs, you have to be ready to provide it.

No, Golden Time can be achieved only when your baby is sleeping for long intervals, thereby allowing you to sleep for long intervals. I remember the realization that Courtney was hitting her stride when it came to sleep. At the time, I was still working the eleven o'clock news and we lived about an hour north of New York City in Westchester.

By the time I got off the train, drove home, let the dog out, and hit the sack, it was about 1 A.M. Courtney timed it so that I would just be hitting my REM sleep stage when she woke up and demanded a bottle at 2 A.M. It worked out to an hour after I hit the pillow. If the news was late and I got to bed at, say, 2 A.M., she'd wake up at 3. It got to the point where I'd just bring the bottle with me and put it on the nightstand. An hour later, her bottle was the perfect temperature thereby saving me a trip back down to the kitchen.

Because of my schedule, I never achieved Golden Time with Courtney during the week. The weekend, however, was another story. Saturdays were what I called "Courtney-Daddy Day." Mommy had her all week, and needed a break to do frivolous things such as regain her sanity, get her hair done, talk to adults— silly activities that kept her from loading up the car and driving to points unknown.

For those of you who have toddlers, you know

what I'm talking about. These tiny versions of us possess the power of speech, mobility, and limited reasoning. They can do just enough to make you crazy. They can't quite dress themselves, but they can tell you that they don't like what you've put them in. They don't like what you've made for lunch, but they don't know what they want. They can get inside the closet and wreck things, but they can't get out.

For most dads, the weekday world of child-raising consists of seeing your babies before you go to work, getting a dose of them before bedtime, and, if Mom is lucky, reading to them and then putting them to bed. The weekend is a concentrated dose of child-rearing and there is no letup. Don't get me wrong, I loved every minute of it with Courtney, but it was relentless.

It was then that I put a name to the feeling that washed over me when I would get her to bed on a Saturday night. It was a more intense version of the feeling that came over me when I had worked really hard that week. I got that paycheck and looked at the net income window and WOW!!! Golden Time!

As I sat in my chair, slowly recovering from the day, my baby asleep in her bed upstairs, that same sensation crept through my being. A sense of accomplishment from doing something you really loved, while at the same time being incredibly tired yet satisfied. Savoring what had transpired earlier, yet being glad it was over with for a little while.

These days, with Leila, Golden Time has taken on new meaning. Now that she's a year and a half, she is motoring from room to room, jabbering nonstop, and keeping Deborah and me on the run. I've extended the time I describe as Golden Time to include the time in the morning that Leila lets us lie in bed and just enjoy being a couple, able to talk about the day ahead and just be.

Suddenly a small voice pierces the silence, signaling that Golden Time is over. A different kind of Golden Time replaces it. Once again, just as with Courtney, a tiny face that lights up when it sees me poke my head in the room fills my heart with pure gold. Who needs Golden Time? All these moments are priceless.

GRANDPARENTS

Recently, I saw my parents in a completely different light. I saw them as grandparents. I had always seen them with my daughters, or the children of my siblings, but this particular weekend was different. Why? Because *I* actually spent time with them as they spent time with Courtney and Leila. Have you ever had an epiphany? A moment when something so elemental, so basic, had eluded you and then suddenly revealed itself to you?

It happened to me this past summer as I watched my folks with my two daughters. I guess I had seen them in action as grandparents, but I had never really watched them, observed them in this role. Heck, they've always been parents to me. Even when I've been in their presence and that of their grandchildren, other things have been going on, obscuring who they are as parents to their children's children.

When I've been at their house, they were being parents—you know, making dinner, talking with daughters and sons and respective significant others, asking the grandkids not to run through the dining room. Other times, the grandchildren were dropped off at my parents' house and we would take off for dinner or a short trip. We didn't get to see them in the act of being grandparents. It was just something I guess I had taken for granted.

I've never taken the actual job of grandparenting for granted, though, maybe because I was so lucky in that department. Say the word *grandmother* or *grandfather* and great memories are conjured up. I truly had "great" grandparents. They're all gone now, but who they were and what they did linger on.

My mother's folks were the kindest, gentlest people you'd ever want to meet. Grandpa Charles Smith was a stout, short man. He was bald with a fringe of gray, wispy hair around his pate. He always reminded me of Fred Mertz on *I Love Lucy*. Everybody who knew him called him "Pop." He was a hobo for a portion of his life, riding the rails and working odd jobs. Then he met my grandmother, Leila, when he was forty years old. She was just twenty-eight, fresh from the island of Jamaica. They fell in love; he landed a steady job and settled down, if you could call owning a house and a car and having nine children settling down.

It was the little things that made him a wonderful grandfather. His overcoat was always filled with pinwheel mints, those little red-and-white mints wrapped in cellophane. He always took the time to talk with his grandkids. He taught me how to dunk graham crackers in cold milk. "Count, Little Al. One one thousand, two one thousand, three one thousand." That was the exact amount of time that your graham cracker could stay in the milk without falling apart. He would come and pick me up on the subway to spend the weekend with him and Grandma Smith.

He always looked the same to me, never aging, never changing. He was a constant in my young life. Until I was about ten, we lived in Brooklyn, while my grandparents lived about forty-five minutes away in Jamaica. I always looked forward to their visits or when we would jump in our station wagon and go visit them. Imagine how excited I was when we moved to another area of Queens, called St. Albans, just a fifteen-minute drive away.

Pop was a huge Yankees fan and could be found during baseball season sitting in his La-Z-Boy, a big stogie clamped in his jaw, rooting for his team, watching the Dumont television in the family room. Many were the times we would pull up to our grandparents' house at dusk, and we could see Pop through the window, sitting in his chair, bathed in the phosphorescent glow of the old Dumont's picture tube, a cigar clenched in his teeth, tip glowing bright with each breath, transfixed by the images of his beloved team. I think he's why to this day I'm a Yankees fan.

My mother shares certain traits with her father. Besides being rabid baseball fans, they both loved to play cards. Even now, my mother's idea of a good time is playing cards while taking a bus trip to Atlantic City. My dad says that as long as the bills are paid and the house isn't repossessed by the bank, her card playing is under control.

Pop loved to come over and play cards. Only problem was, he wasn't very good at it. My mom, on the other hand, was very good. She would wipe Pop out time after time. Once I remember my mother cleaned Pop out and then gave him a buck to take the bus home. Dad took pity on him and drove him back to his house. Since Grandma Smith frowned on card playing, Pop would beseech my mother not to tell "Dearie" about his latest setback. "Dearie" was his pet name for his wife of forty-six years, Leila Yvette Smith. He's been gone now for more than twenty years, and I can honestly say a day doesn't go by that I don't think of him.

His bride, Leila Smith, was a small, quiet

213

woman. She was one of those people who had great powers of observation. She could size up a person in no time flat, yet you would never hear her utter a bad word about anybody.

She called me her "Little Alley Buttons" because I was as cute as a button. Or so she said. I can't quite imagine a ten-year-old chubby kid with glasses and braces as "cute," but I guess that's why she was a grandmother.

I recall sitting at our kitchen table with Grandma Smith while I was still in high school. We were talking about nothing in particular when I asked her if she thought it was ironic that she was originally from Jamaica in the West Indies and here she was, living in Jamaica, New York. "Grandson," she said, "sometimes you have to go a great distance to get back to where you were. Life is like that."

I have an image of her that never varies. Whenever she was at our house, she sat in the corner of the kitchen with a cup of tea and a pair of knitting needles. Her hands were gnarled by arthritis, and yet she still insisted on knitting. When asked why, she would say, "I guess I enjoy the knitting more than the pain."

She was always trying new things. In her eighties, she took up oil painting at her senior center. One of my prize possessions is a small painting of hers—two men in a boat on a beautiful blue ocean. I often look at it and think of her journey across an ocean to discover a country, a husband, and a family. At the age of eighty-two, she was volunteering at the center. "I enjoy working with old folks. They need me," she once told us.

When I was growing up, she labeled me a "chatterbox." She would tell my mother, "Isabel, he is such a chatterbox. He should be on television." I guess the old girl wasn't the only one in the family who could make predictions. Ironically, she passed away six months after I got my first job in television. She was eighty-six years old.

My father's family is from the Bahamas. My grandmother, Remilda, and her husband, Albert, emigrated from Exuma, in the Bahamas, to Miami, and then eventually to New York in 1934. Unfortunately, I never got to know my grandfather. Mental illness kept him institutionalized, and he died when I was young.

I get my sense of ancestry and heritage from my paternal grandmother. Grandma Remilda Roker reveled in her Bahamian roots. She made sure her grandchildren knew where they were from and was the conduit of familial information to and from the islands.

Having a grandmother from the Bahamas had its good and bad sides. The good side was the fabulous yet simple food she would churn out. No matter when we came over to her house, there was always something cooking on the stove or in the oven. Bahamian peas and rice, johnnycake, shrimps and rice, or just chicken in a pot, my grandmother was from the school that said the stockier you are, the healthier you are. Though she would have loved Deborah, she would've thought, Nice girl, but she needs to put some meat on her bones!

The bad side was Grandma Roker's home remedies. She had a cupboard full of roots and weeds from the Bahamas that would cure whatever ailed you. We would avoid coughing or sneezing in her presence at all costs. Otherwise, an errant cough or sneeze would send her into an elixir-making frenzy. One incredibly vile brew was produced from boiling an evil-looking weed called serace. Oddly enough, if we had a cold and were forced to down this disgusting liquid, our illness vanished within a day or so. Years later, while working on a story about homeopathic medicines, I mentioned this root to a botanist I was interviewing. With a knowing smile, he pulled down a huge volume from a shelf and showed me a whole page on the root serace. It turned out my grandmother knew what she was talking about.

A deeply religious woman, she could quote from the Bible, and yet her favorite TV show was *Wheel of Fortune.* She enjoyed herself the most when her family was gathered around her at big family dinners on Thanksgiving or a simple backyard BBQ on the Fourth of July.

During college, I would look forward to receiving care packages from Grandma Roker, boxes filled with cookies, a rum cake, and a Bahamian delicacy called benne. It was a sesame seed candy laced with candied coconut and nuts. My roommates loved it, and begged me to get more. I remember her telling me she was sending me some one time, but I never received it. Turns out my dad had volunteered to mail the package for her, but mysteriously, he never got to the post office. Hmmmmm.

She raised three children on her own and instilled a pride and joy in her grandchildren that her death three years ago, at the age of ninety-two, did little to extinguish.

So it was with this background that I watched—with a mixture of nostalgia and interest—my parents behave as grandparents.

This past summer, I saw them as an older couple being entertained by and entertaining their granddaughters in the house of their son and daughter-in-law. I watched as my dad played Pictionary with Courtney, took her fishing, and, in the time-honored grandfather tradition, slipped her a five-dollar bill when the weekend was over. I watched my mom talk to Courtney about school and friends, and inquire about Courtney's mother and her mother's family. I saw them fight over who would hold their newest grandchild the longest.

I miss my grandparents. I cherish my parents and what they mean to Courtney. And I guess I'm glad I got to see what they mean to her and she to them. I only hope someday Courtney and Leila feel that way about how I treat their children. Which would of course make me a grandfather. YIKES!!! I hope that's a long way off. And it will be, if that birds-and-bees talk I had with Courtney took.

THE GIRLZ

A number of people have asked me, "How is Courtney getting along with her baby sister?" The answer is: wonderfully. I must admit, it was something I was a little worried about. For eleven years, Courtney was the only princess in the house. Suddenly, there was a usurper to the throne. During this whole process, Deborah and I have really worked at making sure Courtney knows she is still a priority in our lives.

"Dad, how can you love Leila as much as you love me?" was a question I fielded more than once during the pregnancy. My answer was and still is, "It's what people do. You love Mom and you love me, right?" And I would get a nod in agreement. "And Nana and Pop-Pop love me and Aunt Alisa and Aunt Desiree and all my other brothers and sisters. It's just how it is. But always remember, you are my first child and no matter how many kids Deborah and I have, nothing will ever change that."

I was about six when I asked my father the same question about forty years ago, when another sibling was about to join our household. He told me, "Son, your mother and I have room in our hearts to love all our children. Just like Grandma Roker loves me and my sisters, and Grandma Smith loves your mother and all her brothers and sisters." I looked at him and I guess I understood, but that was them and this was me. I think he was reading my mind, because then he asked me, "Little Al, do you love me and your mother?" I shook my head yes. Suddenly, I got it. You *could* love more than one person and love them the same. And so that was what I told Courtney. I think the lightbulb clicked on over her head as it did mine.

Deborah, for her part, can say emphatically that with any luck, a little bit of wine, and a nice piece of jewelry, there may be one more—and that's it.

What has been so wonderful is watching all the females in my life bond together. I know that Deborah and Courtney have become much closer. Deborah has never tried to replace Courtney's mother. She has been a shoulder to lean on, an ear to talk to, and whatever else Courtney needs her to be.

Courtney, I think, sees Deborah as more than a friend: a confidante, a sounding board. Someone she can talk to about boys, biology, becoming a teen, and more.

Courtney's relationship with Leila has become closer and closer as our baby has gotten older. Let's face it. For the first few months, babies don't really do much. Those early months, Leila was basically a very cute meat loaf. So it was hard for Courtney to warm up to her.

Suddenly, when Leila was about six months

old, Courtney asked to feed Leila her breakfast. Up until then, she'd hold her for a few minutes or keep an eye on her. Her wanting to feed her was a first. So, I turned over the dish with oatmeal and bananas to Courtney and let her take Leila into the family room. And guess what? She did a great job. So much so that we decided she'd take over feeding chores for the day. But by late afternoon, Courtney asked me if I could take over again. "This is a lot of work, Dad," Courtney informed me. Tell me about it.

I know it doesn't seem like a lot, but it meant worlds to me. My two girls, my babies, were together and bonding. Courtney will be a great resource for Leila. She'll clue her in about boys, music, fashion, and the world in general. Leila will keep Courtney clued in to what kids are doing and give her responsibility. They will both get something from each other, and I get so much from both. I *am* a lucky guy.

Then there's Mom. We hear so much about husbands feeling neglected by their wives when a baby comes into the picture. Well, when it comes to daddies and daughters, I think wives sometimes get left out as well.

There is no denying the bond between a father and his daughter. I look at the faces of my two girls and I see the future. They will eventually fall in love, marry, have kids of their own, and continue the cycle that keeps humans on the planet. They know how to twist big, strong dads around their little fingers.

There are times I think Deborah is some-what jealous of what I share with both Courtney and Leila, but she knows that I love her deeply. She knows that without her, I wouldn't be the object of such affection from two such beautiful girls. It's good to be the king.

A SENSE OF LOSS

A few years ago I had picked Courtney up from school and we were headed into the city. I was driving the way I normally do, not too fast, not too slow, when Courtney said, "Dad, aren't you driving a little too fast?" Then, two min-utes later, she spoke up again with, "Dad, aren't you a little too close to that car?"

It went on like this for the forty-five-minute drive to Manhattan. I was changing lanes too much, I wasn't careful enough. I could've hit this car or that. It was driving me crazy. I couldn't figure out where all this was coming from. It was Deborah who put it all together. Courtney, like every other kid in America, had been bombarded with the news about the death of Princess Diana.

Somebody famous who my daughter could relate to was suddenly gone, killed in a car crash. Well, if Princess Diana could be killed in a car crash, so could Dad, Mom, or Courtney.

Suddenly, the real world intruded into my

221

daughter's world. She and Deborah got up early that Saturday morning after Princess Diana's death, along with 50 million other Americans, to watch a princess being eulogized, sung to, and remembered. Later that day, we talked about death and dying, and how I wasn't planning on doing anything that would endanger us. That's why Dad is trying to get in shape so that he's around for a long time to come.

I realized that Princess Diana's death will be her generation's John F. Kennedy or Martin Luther King Jr. They will remember where they were and what they were doing when they heard the news about the death of Diana. They'll tell their kids how they got up early on a Saturday and watched the funeral and heard Elton John sing. I guess it's a rite of passage, a coming-of-age. It's too bad each generation has to have one.

A year later, we were back in the truck, driving toward Manhattan. Courtney was deeply engrossed in an "Archie" comic book. Yes, Archie, Veronica and Betty, Reggie and Jughead, and all the gang at Riverdale High still go to Pop's Chok-lit Shop. It is amazing to me that each generation discovers Archie. Me, I still can't figure out how he got that cross-hatch in the side of his hair.

Anyway, I saw this young girl sitting there, wearing sneakers and jeans and a cute top, with her hair in a ponytail that reaches down to her back, and I wondered, Where did my baby girl go and when was she replaced by an ad for Old Navy?

Knowing that our time is always too limited to let her hang out with Arch and the gang too long, I snapped out of my reverie to chat with her. I told her about a *Today* show assignment that I thought was pretty cool, but not without some element of danger. I was going to go down in a four-person submarine to look at the *Titanic*.

Now, you've got to understand just how much my daughter and countless millions of other girls her age were in love with that movie. How romantic the movie was, how gorgeous Leonardo DiCaprio was. So I figure I would score some major cool points with my kid with this assignment. Isn't it funny? We spend a good part of our adult lives trying to impress our parents, then we try to impress our kids.

So I was expecting her to say, "Gee, Dad, that is really cool," or words to that effect. Instead she looked at me with these big eyes filled with concern and asked, "Dad, is this safe?" I explained that sure it was, I wasn't going on something where I could get hurt knowingly. She replied, "Dad, it's just that I don't ever want to lose you."

I just about lost it right there. That my sweet little baboo could express this gave me pause about the assignment. When I told Deborah about it, she put the final nail in the coffin, so to speak. "So you would do something that might mean your unborn child will never know her father?"

The fact is, I could be walking down the street and a bus jumps the curb and BAM, it's Roker pâté. So the moral of the story is, we should make sure those near and dear to us know how we feel as often as possible. Do your loved ones know how much they mean to you and how you never want to lose them? I wasn't sure the people around me did. So I make sure they do. Whenever I talk to my folks, I always tell them I love them. When I leave Courtney, she hears me tell her that I love her.

I plan on being around for a long time, but, like they say on the lottery commercial, "Hey, you never know!"

BOYS

It happened about six months ago. A boy called looking for Courtney. He was a boy she knew from summer camp. "Hi. Is Courtney home?" I looked at the receiver as if it were transmitting alien code that contained information about the destruction of our planet and life as we know it. As far as I was concerned, this *was* the destruction of life as I knew it.

A boy was calling my daughter. "Who is this?" I queried. "Uh...this is Rafael, Mr. Roker. Is it okay that I call?" What do you think, Sparky? Is it okay for you to shatter the illusion that my little girl is NOT growing up? That she has NOT started to notice boys, or even more importantly, boys are NOT starting to notice her?"Uh...Mr. Roker, are you there?" This pre-teen male voice with edges of huskiness woke me from my reverie and snapped me back into reality. "No, Rafael, she's not here right now, and yes, it's okay that you call. Tell you what, give me your phone number and I'll tell her you called."

I hung up the phone, shaken. When could this have happened? Have I been asleep for the past year? Or perhaps I've been deluding myself. Now that this veil has been torn from my eyes, I see it so clearly now.

Following the phone call, I decided to be more vigilant. While I was waiting to pick Courtney up from school, I sat in the parking lot, a respectable distance from the middle school entrance. No middle-schooler wants to be seen being picked up by her parent. Very uncool.

I had been told that *all* the parents wait in the parking lot. I suggested that I drive by the entrance to the lot with a hood over my head and the door open so that she could just do a tuck and roll into the truck. My suggestion was met with a glacial gaze that let me know my humor was, shall we say, underappreciated.

Anyway, I'm sitting there when the bell rings and wave after wave of students poured out of every door of the school. The object of my search came into view. There was Courtney walking with a few of her girlfriends, laughing and talking about only who knows what. I widened my gaze to encompass the other kids around her. To my chagrin, there were boys looking at her and her pals. While I had no knowledge of what my daughter and her friends were talking about, I had a pretty good idea what was being passed between those boys.

Luckily, I had my seat belt on, so the momentary urge to get out of the truck and chase them away passed without incident. For her part, Courtney seemed blissfully unaware of the attention being paid to her.

One weekend, I overheard her and her pals talking about some boy she was madly in love with. Thought he was the cutest boy on the planet. Deborah told me that Courtney had told her about him, and that she should let me know that it's no big deal. Why? Because, as it turns out, she hadn't even talked to the kid, she just really, really liked him.

I had to laugh. Seems Courtney and her dad have a lot in common. When I was in seventh grade, I had a mad crush on this girl in my class. Her name was Kim Burrell, and I thought she was the most beautiful girl at St. Catherine of Sienna School in St. Albans. As far as she was concerned, I was the weird kid with glasses who drew caricatures of the nuns.

I had it in my mind that it would be very romantic to hold a vigil outside her window, much as Romeo did. So every evening for about a week, I would take our dog, Happy, for a walk to pine outside my beloved's window. Today I would be branded as a stalker. In 1967, I was just a very weird boy who stood with a scruffy dog, catty-corner from

Kim's house, looking up at her window. Mrs. Burrell finally came outside on the fifth day and shooed me away. She did not see it as romantic. She saw it as annoying. My dog and I saw it as exercise—for Happy, a brisk mile walk; for me, an exercise in futility.

I'm still friends with Kim and we laugh about my attempt at seventeenth-century romance, but that's why I'm not too concerned about a twelve-year-old boy calling Courtney. That's not to say we haven't had "the talk" that parents seem to be having with their kids at a younger and younger age. Courtney listened to what I had to say and then stated for the record that all the people she hangs out with are just friends. I know that, but it's not always going to be that way.

She's far more mature than I was at her age. In fact, I remember my dad and me having the same talk when I was a couple of years older than my daughter. He prefaced it with, "I think you're old enough and mature enough to talk about sex." All I was thinking was, I wonder if we'll finish this in time for me to catch *The Flintstones*?

Vive la différence!

RECITAL FEVER

Courtney, being the typical suburban girl, has taken the usual flight of lessons. From ballet to piano to theater, you name it, she's done it. I'm a big believer in these activities. It gives kids self-esteem, motivation, and, best, something to keep them occupied while Mom and Dad run to the grocery store and the dry cleaners on Saturdays.

And with these classes comes the ritual that I have grown to look forward to more and more each year: the recital. The recital mirrors her growth physically and emotionally. Seven years ago, when she was a bitty one, just five years old, it was so cute watching all these Munchkins basically run onstage, trot around in a circle once or twice, curtsy, bow, then exit, stage left.

That's the best part: watching with pride as your baby performs her little heart out after weeks of practice and lessons. The worst part of these recitals is that you can't leave after your child is done. Let's face it. When your kid is little, she is not the world's greatest singer/dancer/actor. I mean, you think she is and her grandparents think she's the next Rudolf Nureyev or Judith Jamison, but the fact is, she's not.

Once you've seen your child prodigy, what's the point of sitting through and watching the rest of these children who can't possibly measure up to your little genius? But you sit through it. You sit through it because you want to be supportive. You want to be nurturing. And you don't want other people walking out when it's your kid's turn!

Fast-forward to this year. My little girl has become a not-so-little girl. The development in certain areas had begun, and frankly, I wasn't ready for it. I wanted her to stay around six or seven. Why couldn't she remain my little one for just a while longer?

I went backstage before the recital, and I looked right past her. Why? She was wearing makeup, and had her hair all done up. Oh, man. When I finally recognized her, I could see she was talking with her buddies, and did not look especially thrilled to have Dad there.

She, of course, was one of the best ballerinas on stage, executing her number flawlessly. But I realized as we drove home that we were entering a new phase. And it made me sad. I liked the way we were as a father and a daughter. Granted, we don't see nearly enough of each other because of the divorce. But we've settled into a groove that is comfortable for both of us. We talk, we laugh, we enjoy each other's silly jokes.

Then, two years ago, I was telling friends and family that Courtney was in *Grease*. They looked at me quizzically and asked, "What's she doing there? Is she with her mom?" "No, no, no," I explained. "Not Greece! She's in the musical *Grease.*" She took part in a two-week summer theater workshop where she lives, culminating in two performances of *Grease*. I gotta tell you, my kid's got talent. Lord knows, she doesn't get it from her father.

Since this was her first year, she was in the chorus for all the big numbers, and had a more featured chorus role in "Beauty School Dropout." Like every other obnoxiously proud parent, I was there, 35mm and video camera at the ready. As I zoomed in to the stage in search of my child, there was this really good-looking chorus member. Hey, she kind of looks like Courtney...nah, my kid is only eleven years old and very cherubic. This girl has a little figure and is wearing makeup and has the beginnings of being a knockout.

Just at that moment, my dad leans over and whispers, "You're in trouble, Papa. Your little girl's becoming a young woman." I stop taping to look at the stage without the aid of a viewfinder. YIKES!!! That *is* Courtney. And there she is smiling, singing, giggling.

I think my father really enjoyed the moment. He went through it three times with my sisters, and now his son is going through it. A passing of the torch, if you will. Or, in this protective father's case...a passing of the shotgun!!

This past year, she was in *Into the Woods*, playing Cinderella. If you had told me several years ago that Courtney would enjoy being onstage, singing, dancing, and acting, I would've said you were crazy. Now you can't keep her away from it. It's called letting go. I'm willing to let go...in about fifteen or twenty years.

But then there's Leila. She'll be tiptoeing across a stage in a few years. And in case any of your kids are in the same class with my little girl, I am thrilled and delighted to be watching your tiny genius. I would never think about leaving early. And you'd better not either.

PERFORMANCE ANXIETY

There isn't a parent alive who doesn't think that his child is (A) a genius, (B) a prodigy, and (C) the cutest baby to poop in Pampers. As far as I was concerned, Courtney was a gifted reader who possessed perfect pitch and should have been the baby on the Gerber cereal box. Her sister, Leila, has many of the same qualities.

How many of us look at the sports-obsessed parent-coaches of Little Leaguers, AYSO Soccer, and Pop Warner football and roll our eyes thinking we are so beyond pushing our kids to excel in their respective sports? Yet, from the very beginning, we push our babies to be early learners who can recite their ABCs, know their colors, and identify various body parts.

When Courtney was about a year old, right after having her diaper changed and being bathed, she and I would go into drill mode. While I was feeding her, I would point out colors, make animal sounds and give the corresponding animal names, recite the ABCs, and gesture to Daddy's nose...Courtney's nose. Talk about stimulation overload. And why did I do it? Because if, say, her grandparents came over, I wanted to be able to show them just how smart and advanced my Courtney was.

"Sweetie, tell Nana your ABCs," I would coax. Courtney would look at me, then Nana, and proceed to crawl away in search of a dust bunny under the couch or her Big Bird toy under the coffee table. Of course, I was mortified. God forbid anybody should think she was an average child. This was a baby who could recite her ABCs, count from one to ten, and knew four different colors.

Courtney had no idea that her performance was causing me anxiety. Just before we would go to the pediatrician, I would go over her acquired skills so that she would be ready to hit her marks when given the proper prompts. At home she would point to her nose when I asked, "Where's Courtney's nose?" She could count to ten, recite her ABCs, and say *blue* when I held up a blue ball and asked its color. All right, it's show time. She's ready.

I would put her in the car seat and ask her to perform a couple more "tricks" just to keep her warmed up on the drive over to the doctor's. Once inside, I'd make some small talk with the receptionist, and she would comment on how bright Courtney was. I smiled and thanked her, but I wasn't going to put my little prodigy through her paces just yet. I was saving Courtney's best stuff for the doc.

Finally, we would get ushered into an examining room and I'd start undressing my little virtuoso. Her doctor would come in and ask how everyone was, make small talk, and ask cursory questions about Courtney's health. All the while, I was thinking, C'mon, c'mon. Ask how she's developing. Eventually, he would ask, "So, how is Courtney doing? Is she clapping hands, making sounds?" Making sounds? Hah, she can do more than that, pally. "Courtney, show Doctor Handlesman where your nose is," I requested. Courtney looked at me, then at Dr. Handlesman, and scrunched up her face and broke wind. Suddenly I could feel a fine sheen of perspiration develop on my forehead. My baby was choking! "Ha ha ha, like Daddy, like daughter. Okay, sweetie, show Dr. Handlesman the blue ball." Courtney picked up a red block and tossed it at Daddy! Okay, show's over.

I swore then and there that I would not make the same mistake with Leila. She was not going to be a performing baby who would bring pride and glory to her father. Right!

Ask anyone who met Leila about a year ago if I didn't make her do "Where's Leila?" That's where I would put a napkin or a burp towel on her head and say, "Where's Leila?" Leila would then take it and pull it off her head and look at you and I would say, "There she is!" Then I'd say, "Where's Leila?" and my little genius would cover her head with the cloth again. We would go on like this for five minutes. Everyone who saw it was very impressed, but I'm sure they also thought, What a sap. Making his daughter perform parlor tricks.

So today I'm in PA—Performance Anonymous. It's a very nice group. "Hi, my name is Al." "Hi, Al!!!" everyone responds. "It's been three months since I made my daughter moo like a cow in front of her grandparents." The room erupts into applause, making me think about how Leila will clap on cue if I clap. Surely I could get her to do that at her next pediatrician's visit. Uh-oh.

NURTURING THOSE TALENTS

Just before the start of the millennium, there was some author who said that all those classes we baby-boomer parents were schlepping our toddlers to didn't make a difference when it came to nurturing intelligence.

Is this guy nuts? This must've been someone who resented taking his kid to class because it interfered with his golf game on the weekends. I don't care what studies say, you can't tell me that exposing your children to all sorts of ideas and classes doesn't help them.

I have to imagine it's sort of like cultural chicken soup. Maybe it works, and maybe it doesn't, but it can't hurt.

Here in Manhattan, we can take these things to extremes. There are some toddlers who need their own Palm Pilot to schedule all the different classes they go to. Violin, dance, soccer, swimming—you name it, it's offered. But just because it's there doesn't mean your kid has to take it *all*.

Look, Courtney's taken piano, ballet, and theater. As she tried them, some she kept, some she wanted out of. To a certain extent, we've let her choose what she wanted. She isn't a world-class athlete, so I don't push her into sports. When she wants to try out for a team, she'll do it.

Leila has gone to toddler tumbling and a music-play class and seems to enjoy it. We play games both in class and at home, and I must say, she is quite the talented tiny tot. And what parent doesn't look at his baby, see her do something like wave a wooden spoon, and jump to the obvious conclusion that this baby genius is destined to conduct the New York Philharmonic? By the way, Leila will be making her conducting debut on May 22, 2019. Save the date.

I remember how my parents would nurture skills for us. In the late '60s and early '70s, Black Power and Afro-centric pride were front and center in the African-American community. Our little corner of Queens was no exception. My folks decided that all three of my sisters would take African dance classes that a neighbor of ours was offering. Ms. Frances Rhymes was a former professional dancer who lived in St. Albans and ran a dance school at a neighboring Catholic church parish center. Saturdays were taken up with shuttling the girls to and from St. Benedict De Moor's Parish Center for beginning, inter-mediate, and advanced African and inter-pretive dance.

Since my mother didn't drive, my father had to perform the shuttle bus duties in our Country Squire station wagon. Once again, here was a man who spent forty to fifty hours a week driving a bus. So what did he have to do for most of Saturday? Drive what was essentially a mini-bus full of girls to dance class. And since the classes were just about flush up against each other, he was stuck there.

Imagine his supreme joy when his oldest son, Albert, got his driver's license at sixteen. Of course, I was not exactly overjoyed with the prospect of spending *my* Saturdays at the Frances Rhymes African and Interpretive Dance School. But my father made a powerful argu-ment to convince me to take over the dance shuttle. One Saturday morning at the breakfast table he said, "You want to use the car tonight?" Duhhh. "Sure, Dad," I answered tentatively. "Well, then, there are a couple of things you need to do today." Suddenly I saw where this was going, and I didn't like the route. "Here are the car keys. Take your sisters to dance class." Talk about a pact with the Devil. But I wanted that car, so I reluctantly took the keys as my sisters came barreling down the stairs in leotards and ballet slippers. Grrrreat.

But it was all in the name of nurturing their talent. And my parents made the investment in their children's future not only temporally but financially as well. At the time, my father was a bus driver and had five kids in Catholic school. It couldn't have been easy, yet he did it. He worked extra shifts, took odd jobs, and even ran a restaurant of sorts.

He and a couple of his buddies ran a makeshift lunchroom at the bus depot in between their own bus routes. They had a thriving little enterprise, making sandwiches and hot lunches for other drivers, mechanics, and transit workers at the Fifth Avenue Depot. I really do believe I've inherited a lot of my more creative talents from my dad. Cooking, cartooning, and writing are just a few of the skills I think Albert Sr. passed on to his son.

As a child, I showed a real interest in movies and television. My mother told me that at the age of six I described television programs in terms of "wet" or "dry." When she asked me to explain what I meant, she says I told her a "dry" TV show was either live or videotaped, while a "wet" show was a program that was on film. To me, film had a liquid feel to it, as opposed to a live or videotaped show, which had a crisper quality.

To nurture this, my dad purchased a secondhand Bell & Howell 8mm movie camera from a passenger on his bus route when I was ten years old. It was like manna from heaven. I began filming everything—family gatherings, neighborhood scenes, even the television. I became fascinated with film, but especially with animation. I loved animated cartoons. My father would come home from work and would watch "Huckleberry Hound," "Quick Draw McGraw," and "Tom and Jerry" with me. He found a book on animation for me called *Cartoon Animation* by Disney and MGM animation veteran Preston Blair.

Eventually, I was down in our basement making crude black-and-white, two-minute animated cartoons. I experimented with stop-action films, using store-bought Gumby and Pokey figures. From there, I became interested in film comedy. Laurel and Hardy, Abbott and Costello, the Three Stooges, and Buster Keaton became my heroes. Before the days of home video, you could purchase theatrical releases for home viewing, especially short subjects, comedies, and cartoons.

To finance my hobby, I began cutting lawns and baby-sitting. After all, I had to buy a projector, a screen, and editing equipment. My parents subsidized me when they could, supporting what they saw as a creative outlet for their son. I was not a very athletic child. One of the few times I took part in softball, I was chasing down a ball and slipped on it and went down facefirst. I broke my two front teeth and scraped up my face pretty badly. They knew instinctively that they did not have a Hank Aaron or a Willis Reed on their hands.

My dad picked up a secondhand reel-to-reel tape recorder for me as well. Sound and picture went hand in hand, and just about the time I became interested in movies and television, radio became an interest as well. At eleven years old, I started placing a microphone in front of the TV speakers to record audio from shows we would watch, but it sounded hollow and picked up noise in the room. Then I figured out how to get the cover off the TV and hook up the leads from the television speakers to the line-in input of the tape recorder. I could now record sound directly from the television. It was like some great discovery, and I began recording and cataloging sounds from my favorite TV shows.

God bless my mother. I would lug this twenty-pound tape recorder around the house, playing my latest recordings for her. "Listen, Mom...Superman!" And my mother would listen intently and tell me, "That's great, dear." I know now how I drove her crazy, but she was nurturing one of her child's interests.

My oldest sister, Alisa, has told Courtney and her children how I would ask her and my brother innocuous questions like "Do you like ice cream?" "Do you like doing homework?" They'd respond with the appropriate yes or no. Then I'd rerecord my questions: "Do you think Mom and Dad are dumb?" and "Do you really listen to Mom and Dad?" And then I'd splice their original answers to the new questions, play it for them, and threaten to play it for Mom and Dad. I was able to extort a couple of extra servings of dessert out of 'em.

I can honestly say I am on TV today because my parents nurtured what many folks might have dismissed as an obsession at best and an unhealthy interest at worst. Odds are that I might not even be doing this today, but they gave me the opportunity and supported it. There were no studies or research that told them to do it. They just did what common sense told them. What a dangerous concept.

A GREAT FATHER'S DAY

Remember when you were a kid and had no disposable income for gifts? Instead, you made stuff for your folks on their birthday or Father's Day.

Well, I had a great Father's Day last year. Besides getting to celebrate the day with both of my girls, Courtney gave me something very special. She made the appropriate Father's Day card, and got me a wonderful gift. But the best part of the day was what she made me for lunch.

About a month ago, we were all talking about what our favorite dishes were when we were kids. Deborah told Courtney about something her mom made, and I described, in detail, the hard-boiled egg sandwiches my mother used to make for us. Courtney took in every detail. I guess she saw the rapture that enveloped me as I told her about this simple sandwich.

Mom would take one slice of Wonder bread, or any equivalent white bread. You know it's the right bread if you can take a whole loaf and squish it into a one-inch square.

She would take that slice of Wonder and smear it with mayo. Then Mom would make two perfectly hard-boiled eggs. While they were still warm, she'd slice them onto the bread, lightly sprinkle with salt and pepper, then top it with one more mayo-laden slice of Wonder bread. That was good eating!!

So Courtney decided that that was what she was going to make for her dad for Father's Day. She enlisted Deborah's help, and it was great. And watching her watch me eat it was the best Father's Day present I could ever get.

Since Deborah helped Courtney with my present, next year I'm going to tell Courtney about the year my mother made me a brand-new Porsche.

HAPPY BIRTHDAY

On November 17, 1999, Leila celebrated her first birthday. It was a quiet affair, just us and a couple of friends to sing "Happy Birthday" and cut a small cake to mark the day.

If I've learned anything from experience, it's that a big birthday party for a one-year-old is a BIG mistake. First of all, a one-year-old has NO idea what's going on. All she knows is that there are a whole lot of people around, making a whole lot of noise.

After a while, the baby senses some sort of crescendo—people singing, or to them, yelling about some Bird Day. Then this round thing with flames coming out of it appears, and Mommy and Daddy scoop the baby up, hover over the flaming circle, puff a lot, and then the lights go out. Now, wrapped boxes show up, and everyone goes "oooooh" and "aaaaah" each time the paper comes off one of the boxes. The baby wants the paper and the box, but Mom or Dad keeps forcing some toy in front of the baby for a picture. After a while, the baby gets overstimulated, eats too much cake or ice cream, throws up, then has trouble going to sleep.

All in all, after having lived through this with Courtney, I vowed not to make the same mistake twice. Hence, the very understated birthday party six months ago, where we almost outnumbered the guests.

An hour later, everyone was gone and Leila was asleep. Deborah sat next to me on the couch in our family room and said, "You seem a little down this evening. What's bothering you?" I guess I *was* feeling down. It was a feeling that had crept up on me, sort of like my underwear. One minute you're feeling good, and the next minute cotton and elastic have found their way into your nether regions.

While Deborah went and got ready for bed, I sat and pondered. At first, I denied it. What could possibly be wrong? After all, my little girl had just turned one, and by all accounts, she was as good as a one-year-old could be. She was walking. She called me by name. "DA! DA!" she exclaimed when she wanted my attention. She was intelligent, beautiful, spunky, and full of personality. Leila was a healthy, normal, fun-loving one-year-old. So why did I feel melancholy?

The feeling dogged me into my shower and during my evening shave. I got into bed and looked at Deborah and it hit me. "Leila is one,"

I exclaimed. "And you don't want her to be one, do you?" Deborah answered. As usual, my beautiful wife hit the nail right on the head.

I didn't want her to grow up. I did it, Deborah did it, and Courtney's in the middle of doing it. I've already told you how guilty I am of keeping Courtney at a certain age and not wanting her to leave that comfort zone. For the longest time, even though intellectually I knew her to be eight or nine, in my heart I still longed for her to be six or seven. I loved how she was at those ages. And as I finally embraced her real chronological age, I grew to hold that period dear to my heart. I have been dragged screaming and kicking into my older daughter's adolescence.

As kids get older, the parties get more elaborate, the themes become more varied. Courtney's fourth birthday party was a bumper bowling party. Bumper bowling is a wonderful idea, actually. I wish I could do it. Inflatable bumpers are placed in the gutter lanes and smaller, lighter balls are used for smaller, lighter children.

With the bumpers in place, it is impossible for kids to roll a gutter. Every time the ball rolls down the alley, at least one pin gets knocked down. The kids are happy, the parents are happy, and, most important, the party takes place outside your domicile. This guarantees the safety and security of your home against marauding bands of four- and five-year-olds.

A couple of years later, the party du jour was at these giant indoor theme parks like Discovery Zone. I liked this one the best. If you planned it right, this was a kids' *and* parents' dream come true. Courtney's seventh birthday was held at one of these. Her mother and I planned it for four o'clock. Children play for one hour. Nonstop screaming, running, and jumping. Now it's 5 P.M. We moved from the play area, where the kids were still bouncing off walls and hurling themselves into pits of multicolored balls, to a private party room where stacks of hot pizza awaited.

Pizza disappeared down the gullets of twenty-five ravenous children, followed by cake, ice cream, and present opening. There's another hour. Now, you're at 6 P.M. The kids get another hour of play back in the maelstrom that is Discovery Zone. Courtney and her pals were delirious. By 7 P.M., still hopped up on adrenaline and sugar from the cake and ice cream, Courtney was in the car heading home. By 7:30 she was hosed off, in her pj's, being read a story. By 8 P.M. she was sawing logs, another satisfied birthday customer. That, my friends, is the way to run a party.

Now it's sleepovers, with nail painting, music, and boy talk. The party favors, the clowns, and the cute cakes are all a thing of the past. I hate to admit it, but I will miss it. Courtney's parties will be marching toward becoming adult events. Soon her celebrations will center around friends and not her family. Eventually, when she's old enough to appreciate what it all means, her mother and I will be back to help celebrate the annual passage of time.

I guess I had hoped that the normal progression of life would somehow miraculously skirt Leila, allowing her to remain in this pretoddler stage a little longer than necessary. I love our nonverbal conversations when it's time for bed. Her tiny arms wrap themselves around my shoulders as best they can and she holds on for all she's worth. I love her giggles as I pull her diaper off, her laugh when I hold her upside down.

It all changes as she gets older. They are all good changes, but different. The hug I get from Courtney when I leave her on a Sunday night is as good as it gets. There are times I never want to let go of her. Maybe when I do, she will be my little girl again, wanting nothing more than to go see *The Little Mermaid* or *Aladdin*, instead of *Scream 7: The Retirement Years*.

I got out of bed and went into Leila's room to look at her sleeping. There she was, stretched out in her crib. As my eyes adjusted to the dark, I could see her tiny fingers holding her Winnie the Pooh stuffed cube, breathing to a rhythm set by angels.

We have no idea how our babies are going to turn out, do we? As I looked down into that crib I almost got dizzy thinking about everything there is to come: school, friends, heartache, dating, college, marriage, babies, and her crazy old father to deal with. All that lay ahead of this sleeping cherub. North of Manhattan, an intelligent, beautiful teenager is wrestling with coming-of-age, boys, friends, and impending high school.

This truly is an adventure, one I wouldn't trade for anything. And with any luck, while Deborah's guard is down, maybe we can start another adventure. Gotta go!